MOSTLY SUNNY

MOSTLY SUNNY

HOW I LEARNED TO KEEP SMILING
THROUGH THE RAINIEST DAYS

JANICE DEAN

HARPER

NEW YORK · LONDON · TORONTO · SYDNEY

HARPER

FIRST HARPER PAPERBACKS EDITION PUBLISHED 2020.

Designed by Bonni Leon-Berman

Library of Congress Cataloging-in-Publication Data has been applied for.
ISBN 978-0-06-287758-1
20 21 22 23 24   LSC   10 9 8 7 6 5 4 3 2 1

To my husband, Sean

I still wake up at night sometimes feeling I am alone in this world.

And then I smile because I know you're right next to me.

Each step and every breath has guided my way

To finding you.

And the beautiful family we have made

Together

In love.

CONTENTS

MOSTLY SUNNY

PROLOGUE

"Hey, what's your name? Where ya from? What do you think of the weather today?" I was smiling, hand on my hip, nodding my head, giving her a cue to talk into my microphone. I wanted to learn about where she was from and see if she could give me a quick sentence about the weather we were having.

"I'm Melanie. From Ottawa. Janice, you already know this!"

"But just *pretend* I'm a reporter!" I pleaded. "Make something up. You're on TV!"

"But I'm not on TV. And that's not a microphone. That's a large spoon. C'mon, let's go get our bikes and go to the playground."

This was my audience . . . my friend Melanie. The place we were make-believe broadcasting from? My front yard.

That was over forty years ago. Today I'm doing the same thing with my friends that come to visit me outside of the *Fox & Friends* studio in midtown Manhattan, where I do weather in the morning. Now I have a real microphone and camera in front of me broadcasting live to an audience of millions on the number one cable news channel in America.

Not bad for a girl raised in Ottawa, Ontario, Canada. When I moved to New York City in September 2002, it made the headlines of my hometown newspaper, the *Ottawa Citizen*.

I have that page framed. It hangs proudly in my office at Fox News.

I was born in Toronto, Canada, on May 9, 1970. The day I came into the world the headline in the newspaper announced that "President Nixon sends troops into Cambodia—the first expansion of the war in the Far East." That's what my dad wrote in my baby book that I keep in a box under my bed.

We moved to Ottawa, Canada's capital city, shortly after I was born. One of my favorite stories I love to hear my mom tell is when she and my dad went to the Ottawa airport with me when I was a baby. Pierre Trudeau, Canada's prime minister, was flying to Russia, and the Canadian press was surrounding him. My mom caught his eye, and he came right over to chat with her while I was looking around at all the bright lights. (Some things never change.) He asked her if she might want to go with him to Russia, and she motioned to me and said she had her hands full. I have a picture of that exchange with my mom and Pierre Trudeau. It's like folklore in my family. My dad was standing right next to her, but Mr. Trudeau clearly had eyes on her. My mom tells me that at the time, Margaret Trudeau was pregnant with Justin (Canada's current prime minister, son of Pierre), so I like to joke that Justin Trudeau could've been my stepbrother at one point. It was my first brush with the press, and my eyes are on Trudeau. It looks like I'm smiling at him in the glow of the camera's bright lights.

My mom, Stella, was born in St. John's, Newfoundland, the most easterly province in Canada. She was a British subject before Newfoundland joined the confederation with Canada in 1949.

Mom lost her dad when she was very young in a tragic train accident that left my grandmother—her mother—a widow with six children. She had to grow up very quickly, being the oldest sibling—to help care for her brothers and sisters, the youngest of whom at the time was just a baby. They were very poor, but what they lacked in money they compensated for with being a close-knit family. She is still in constant touch with all of her brothers and sisters, most of whom live in and around Toronto.

After Sean and I were married, I brought him to St. John's to see where my mom grew up. There was a big family reunion and we had a wonderful time sightseeing and meeting all the "Newfies" I'm related to. It was funny to see him try to figure out what they were all saying in their rich, animated Newfoundland accents. He also went through a famous ceremony of being "screeched" in—a traditional way of becoming an honorary Newfie. There's only a handful of bars that perform the ritual and you get a membership certificate for taking part. The key assignments require taking a shot of the screech—a somewhat drinkable rum, although it's pretty gross—and then you kiss a dead cod on the lips. It's not for the faint of heart. You may have to recite something as well, depending on how organized the bar is that does the swearing in.

My mom moved to Toronto in her early twenties to work for Air Canada. She met my dad at a wedding reception of a mutual friend in Mississauga, Ontario (outside of Toronto), in November 1968. They almost didn't meet, because Stella never got the invitation, and it was a last-minute party crash on my mom's part. My father was there on the groom's side—an American from Toledo, Ohio. They met, enjoyed each other's company, and my dad suggested he come to Toronto the following weekend. They were married six months later.

He and my mom were together for twenty-five years before he left. When he was home, I was so happy. He worked a lot, so weekends when he wasn't still at the office were a treat. I still remember him teaching me to ride a bike like it was yesterday. He pushed me off without my training wheels, and I started pedaling. I could hear him in the background:

"Go, Pookie! Go! You're doing it! You're doing it!"

My dad was strikingly handsome and, when he wanted to be, very charming. He could tell a great story and made people laugh. However, he could also be distant, moody, and reclusive.

My father was a workaholic, spent a lot of time by himself when he was at home, and had a lot of social phobias. My mom used to tell me he would find friends, and they would hit it off, and then he would think they were backstabbing him or talking behind his back. He would never speak with them again.

Dad was off-the-charts smart. He knew back in the late 1970s that we would be ordering things off of computers one day and told this to anyone who would listen. He had a home computer before anyone else did in the '80s. My father was fascinated by science fiction and had seen the movie *2001: A Space Odyssey* at least a dozen times when it first came out and was panned by critics. My mom says when they were dating he spent an hour explaining the entire movie to her. She wasn't too keen on it, but she did like him quite a bit.

My dad is the reason why I have my American citizenship. When he met my mom and they got married, they moved to Toronto and he became a Canadian citizen. Years later, in 1987, during the time when the Canada–US Free Trade Agreement was reached, my mom saw a small article in Toronto's *Globe and Mail* that stated if you were an American who gave up your citizenship, you could now get it back and, in doing so, you could also apply for citizenship for your children. My dad always thought he had forfeited his US citizenship when he moved to Canada, but it's unclear if that's the case. In any event, without that free trade agreement, I don't think I would be here. It was a very long process. He needed to prove that he lived in the US for twenty years and had to get letters from schools and old friends and show proof that he had worked in the Air Force. My mom says it helped a great deal that he wasn't a draft dodger.

I remember the mound of paperwork he had to fill out for me, and I will always be grateful for that. He was going to do the same for my brother, Craig, but things got complicated, and he left my mom before he ever could start the process for him.

Two years ago, I did a DNA test on *Fox & Friends* and received more information on my father's side of the family than I could've ever hoped for. My dad has incredibly strong roots in the US. My direct ancestor Isaac Dean was born in 1782 in Pennsylvania. My great-grandfather Howard L. Dean, whom my dad was named after, was a salesman and was born in Ohio. In his World War I draft registration card from September 1918, it says that he was tall with gray eyes and blond hair. My grandfather Roy Ambrose Dean was a technical observer in the 8th US Army in 1946 and then worked for Coca-Cola.

When the MyHeritage people presented this information to me live on *Fox & Friends*, I had tears in my eyes, because strangely I felt closer to my father than I had in decades. I mourned our fractured and distant relationship in the end.

I get my drive and ambition from my dad. He could do anything he set his mind to. He owned his own construction business in Toledo and Ottawa for a few years. With all his computer knowledge, he decided to call himself a systems engineer, even though he never technically went to school to learn engineering. He was a contractor who helped design communications infrastructure for museums in Canada and in New York. My father also loved politics and volunteered with the Progressive Conservative Party in Canada to help elect Prime Minister Joe Clark. I helped stuff envelopes with my dad during his campaign and received a handwritten note from the prime minister himself thanking me for my support in his election. I have it saved in my box of mementos under my bed.

I couldn't wait to get to the age where I could work, so as soon as I turned fourteen, I went to Dad to help me with my first résumé. He loved the challenge of figuring out how we were going to create something with so little job experience. Since I did help stuff letters during a campaign season, we included this. I wish I still had that old résumé. We may have embellished the truth a bit to make it look like I had quite the little career at the age of fourteen. I think we may have even included the fact that I won first place in a school science fair when I was ten.

My first job was at a clothing store called Dapper Dan's in Bayshore Shopping Centre in Ottawa. I remember being dazzled by the neon lights and the '80s bright colors. It was the main reason I wanted to work there. I couldn't wait to fill out that job application. My dad made that résumé look like it belonged to someone who had been working for years. He printed it out on expensive linen paper, and it was beautifully typed. I was called in for a job interview and they hired me on the spot despite the fact that I was only fourteen. The manager, Deb, said she liked my enthusiasm. I could work a maximum of only twelve hours a week per Canadian government work regulations.

I was a pretty thin kid until I was about eight or nine, when I started to gain weight. Before that, I was active, enrolled in swimming, figure skating, and ballet. One day I told my mom I didn't want to do any of it. My hobby then became eating, and it didn't take long for my love of food to catch up to me. I was teased at a young age about being overweight, and I've always carried a little more around my hips, thighs, and backside.

My mom started to worry about how I was being teased in school, so she took me to a pediatrician to get some advice on how to help me. I remember the doctor saying I had something called a "fat gene" that made me more prone to being overweight. I was so ashamed. I had to go to the "husky girls" section of the clothing stores to get things to fit. The husky girls never had cute jeans or dresses like the "normal" girls in my class. Very recently, I was in a department store and saw the "husky kids" section, and I immediately felt shame from all those years ago.

I couldn't stand to look at myself in the changing room mirror and heard one salesclerk even say, "She has such a pretty face. If she lost some weight, she would be perfect."

I went to Weight Watchers when I was in high school. My mom shopped for all the special foods and tried to cook recipes that helped me lose weight. I ate a lot of plain hamburgers with low-fat cheese for several weeks. It worked for a while, and people were telling me I looked *great*. But that didn't last. I was back into my huskies in no time.

Most of the teasing came because of my weight—but then I was mocked for different things as well, to mix it up. There were mean girls in my class who would laugh every time I would read out loud. They would whisper, "She has the most terrible voice!" I find it quite satisfying that my career was later based on that awful voice they were so horrified to hear. However, at the time it made me even more self-conscious and shy to speak. I had one kid spit at me on a daily basis when I got on the bus. For all those days I couldn't say anything to him out of fear, allow me to have a moment (his name was Neil; I haven't changed the name to protect him):

YOU SUCK, NEIL!

There were many days I never wanted to go to school because of the teasing and mean comments.

It was such a dark time in my life, being heavy and not able to control myself. I remember seeing my mom hiding the sweets one day so I wouldn't find them—so when she would be out of the house, I would pull up a kitchen chair to the highest cupboard, stand on the counter, and find the cakes and cookies and eat all of them.

At my heaviest, I think I was probably over 200 pounds. I would wear the same long, extra-large men's jean jacket every single day to hide my growing waistline.

It wasn't until late in high school and my first year of university that I decided to cut back on my eating. I lost about 50 pounds in less than a year. It wasn't healthy the way I lost weight, and I probably had an eating disorder. I would count calories and limit myself to an oatmeal muffin top for breakfast, a ham sandwich for lunch, and not much for dinner.

Finally, I was losing weight and I felt more people paying attention. The rude comments, whispers, and stares were becoming less frequent. I always had boys who were my good friends in school, but never any that liked me as a possible "girlfriend." I felt things changing around me. One of my close male friends who I never in a million years would've dreamed could like me in "that way" once leaned over while we were doing a school project and tried to kiss me. I was shocked and pulled away. He was embarrassed and never tried anything again, but I knew that suddenly I was more attractive to boys. The only thing that was different was I was smaller. That was a powerful feeling. I had never, at that point, kissed a boy.

Suddenly, I was being asked out on dates, and I was able to fit into clothes I had never thought I could fit into. I remember shopping with a girlfriend, and she was looking at jeans. I hadn't bought a pair of jeans in a decade and had no idea what size I was. She told me to try on a 5/6. (I probably weighed 130 pounds, and at five-eight that's very thin for me.) I laughed and told her I could probably only get an ankle in and never make it up to the knee. I couldn't believe my eyes when I buttoned them up. I was shocked. She asked me to come out of the changing room so she could see me. I hesitated, still feeling like the fat girl, but I got the courage to leave the four walls that protected me from feeling bad about myself. I walked out into the bright lights of the store and the salespeople and shoppers. My friend was so happy for me. "Look at you. You look like a supermodel!"

I remember going on a trip with my closest childhood friend, Neera, to Cancún one year and wore a bikini for the first time since I was a toddler. My mom was picking us up at the airport. The first thing she said was "Janice, you look emaciated!" I didn't know what that meant, but if it meant skinny, then I was #winning.

I kept the emaciated look up for a while, and even tried out for something I never believed I could do in a million years: I entered a contest for "Face of the '80s," a modeling competition in Ottawa. They had a booth set up at one of the shopping malls downtown where I had my picture taken and filled out a form asking my height and weight. I never won first prize but was a runner-up, which means I was encouraged to take a course with the modeling agency that was looking for said "'80s faces." It was so exciting to learn how to put on makeup, do my hair, and "walk the runway." I loved getting pictures taken, but the runway wasn't my strong suit. I hated changing in front of everyone when we had to do fashion shows. Even though I was thin, I still felt ashamed of my body.

I don't have many pictures of myself from when I was heavy. I threw a lot of them away and hate being reminded of the days I was teased and bullied. Even writing this, I feel that shameful wave come over me again about the way I look. I still struggle every day with what I eat, although now I'm a little forgiving about what the scale has to say. Now that I'm a mom and have kids, I try to eat well and exercise—and by that I mean walking as much as possible and taking the stairs when I can. Hey, it adds up!

My boys are now getting to the age at school where they are beginning to realize what bullying is like, whether they see other kids being teased or they themselves feel like they are the target of some mean kids' comments. Both Matthew and Theodore get upset when I tell them stories of how I was teased in school for my weight. Theodore's face turns red with anger and he says, "I wish I could've been there to protect you. I would yell at those terrible kids!" Matthew tears up instead and says: "I feel so bad for you when you were little, Mama."

My sweet boys.

I tell my kids that sometimes people bully because they are jealous of us; sometimes it's because people don't feel good about themselves; sometimes it's because they're just plain mean. I've told them to let me know when someone isn't nice to them, and we'll talk it through. If I need to talk to their parents, I will. If we need to go to the teacher or principal, we will do it together. I tell them sometimes it's okay to ignore the mean comments, but if it continues, we have to say something. Sometimes we have to stand up for ourselves.

Chapter 1

READY, SET: PERFORM!

Despite my fluctuating waistline, from a young age I loved to perform. It was like I could be another person, and all my troubles would disappear. For a few minutes the spotlight was on me, and I would try to command an audience!

I do believe broadcasting is in my DNA. Before I could even read, I memorized *Alice in Wonderland* and would recite it into my dad's huge tape recorder. I would ask him to rewind and replay it for me so I could hear myself talk through his gigantic headphones. I loved performing even at an early age. One of my earliest memories "onstage" was singing "Raindrops Keep Fallin' on My Head" in kindergarten with my class. (Talk about an early hint of what was yet to come!) I auditioned for the school choir with one of my favorites, "You Light Up My Life," with piano accompaniment. I also recall singing along with Carol Burnett's version of "Little Girls" as Miss Hannigan in the movie *Annie*.

In high school I had starring roles in plays and won a few "air band" competitions. (This is an overlooked talent that requires perfect lip-synching to songs. It may sound easy, but it is a skill, my friends.)

One year, I performed Marilyn Monroe's famous "Diamonds Are a Girl's Best Friend" with a few of my male swimmer friends in tuxedoes, including a dance number we invented. My mom loves to tell the story about how three handsome, blond, athletic young men would come to our house and practice our routine down in the basement.

A few of my girlfriends decided we should be the Pointer Sisters the following year and we performed three different songs with dance routines for each number. We practiced like crazy, borrowed outfits from someone's mom, and won first prize. I loved the rush of adrenaline you get from performing in front of a crowd. We also got to do our award-winning performance on a local television program, which of course we all thought (back in the '80s) was totally awesome.

When it came time to figure out what I was going to do after high school, I took one of those career tests, and "journalism" came up as one of my suitable jobs. That, and flight attendant as a close second. So when it was time to apply for university, I kept it simple and stayed close to home. Carleton University was in Ottawa, and they had an excellent journalism program. I applied and was accepted.

I hated it.

One of the main reasons I was discouraged was I had to wait until fourth year to learn how to be a reporter and get out in the field and file stories. I found out the first three years were filled with subjects and lessons I had decided would mean nothing in the greater scheme of things. I also disliked being one of thousands of students in this huge school. I felt like just a number. No one would get to know me as a person. We were like an assembly line of young adults moving from classroom to classroom like a herd of cattle.

Before realizing that journalism school wasn't for me, I had an assignment that I did enjoy researching and writing about. We were asked to pick a pivotal moment that played an important role in broadcast history. I decided to write a paper on how the Nixon-Kennedy televised debate on September 26, 1960, changed American politics. I think my dad suggested it. I was fascinated when I started reading about it. This was the first televised presidential debate in US history, and it had a major impact on the outcome of the election. It showed the important role television was about to play in the decades to come. Mr. Kennedy was the handsome, young, Irish-American senator and by the end of the night he was a star.

I had read that people who listened to the debate on the radio between the candidates thought Nixon had won, but those who had watched television decided it was the youthful, healthy-looking Kennedy who did better. Mr. Kennedy had a wide smile, and a tan that he worked on during debate prep. He also had a makeup artist touch him up before the debates. Meanwhile, Nixon was pale: he had been sick and didn't look well. He also refused the makeup artist. (Oh, my!)

Senator Kennedy knew how important this television appearance would be and came out looking like a movie star. Richard Nixon treated it like just another campaign appearance and looked like hell.

I spent hours researching and writing this essay. This was before the Internet, so that required going to the library and finding books and print articles. I loved the drama behind the story.

By the way, my former boss, Roger Ailes, was the one that eventually helped Nixon win the 1968 presidential election after he was hired to be his executive producer for television. Nixon had learned from his mistakes, thanks to Mr. Ailes, who coached him to become a better performer and even created a series of televised roundtables called *The Richard Nixon Show*.

Throughout my academic life, I was used to getting good grades without a whole lot of study or prep time, so when I received a C+ on my Nixon-Kennedy paper I had spent so much time on, I was furious. I felt like this was a total waste of my time. Of course, it is also worth noting that during this period I had a boyfriend who was moving to California. I was distracted by this unfortunate development in my social life. I was only in journalism school for a few months when I announced I was going to take a year off. I had heard of a few of my friends doing this as a way of "finding themselves" before going back to school and focusing on the rest of their lives. I also wanted to work and make money—maybe travel a bit. (California was calling my name.) My parents were not impressed, but they didn't argue with me too much. They trusted I would figure it out . . . somehow.

Chapter 2

"BYLAW BASE TO CAR 16!"

Then came a series of jobs that started to get my wheels turning about what my career path might eventually look like.

For several years, during the summer, I worked at City Hall in the bylaw enforcement department. I answered phones, took complaints, and filed paperwork. The job was fun, but more importantly I loved the crew I worked with. I came back several summers to help out in the office. In Canada, bylaws are noncriminal rules, laws, or regulations that are enacted by the local government. I like to refer to this as basically all the stuff the cops don't want to do. Examples of such enforcement issues would be dogs on the loose, dog licensing, neighbors complaining about dogs, dogs barking, long grass or weeds, noise complaints, building permits, and parking tickets. I would take calls, write down complaints, and eventually type them into the computer. It was a fascinating study in human behavior. Many complaints came in from the same people, who would snitch on their neighbors. I recognized their voices when they called in.

There was one year where we even tried to license cats. No explanation needed here. Try putting a leash on a cat. Good luck.

I loved the staff there, including one of the secretaries, named Elaine, who would make me laugh all day long. The officers were funny too; sometimes we would make up little inside jokes while talking to each other on the dispatch radio. I would use my best broadcasting voice to let them know their next job after a complaint was filed:

"BYLAW BASE TO CAR 16. THERE'S A 10–36 ON THE LOOSE." (There was a whole list of codes for violations.)

"Roger that, JD. Location?"

"Last spotted corner of Richmond and Lorry Greenberg. Black Lab."

"10–4 on the K-9."

Elaine used to tell me that when I started my career in radio, it was my dispatching calls from the bylaw department that started it all.

When I abruptly quit university, taking a year of "Janice," I called Elaine to see if they needed extra help in the bylaw office. I told her my plan: a year off school to figure stuff out. I also needed to make money to buy a plane ticket to see my long-distance boyfriend, Tom. Elaine suggested I apply to be an actual uniformed officer since they made more money; it would be full-time. I already knew all the laws, having worked in the office for several years during the summer. Some of the officers were doing the job while going to school, so that was always an option when I decided to go back. I was not exactly thrilled at my long-term prospects of this as a career, but I liked the concept of being full-time and making more money. So I put on my gray polyester uniform with my clip-on tie, bought a comfortable pair of black sneakers that nurses often wore, and went out on the road.

Let's just say I wasn't the best bylaw enforcement officer. I would get calls to catch dogs and never find them (even if they were right across the street from me, barking at the neighbor). Most times I got yelled at while writing out parking tickets by angry people who had just parked in no-parking zones:

"I was here just for a MINUTE, I swear, to run in to pick something up! *Why are you writing that ticket?*"

I hated going into businesses to tell them their building permits had expired. No one liked seeing the bylaw people. Plus, I was a terrible driver, and this was back when there was no GPS, so you had to rely on maps to get from point A to point B. And, despite trying to look cute in my bylaw enforcement uniform, I found it to be hot and itchy. So I turned in my uniform but kept working that year in the office. Thankfully, during this two-week stretch, in my polyester pants I got someone to take my picture just in case a few decades later I would need to prove that I did this job. (And perhaps include it in a book someday! Ha!)

Although I had fun and was making steady money, I felt like I wasn't doing what my heart desired. My dad always used to say to me when it came to my career:

"Janice Anne, do what you most love to do, and it will never feel like work."

This was not it.

One night I was invited to a restaurant opening after the owners came into City Hall to apply for their business permit. They were young and attractive gentlemen and passed along the invitation to a few of the women in the office. I ended up going and met a guy named Rich who was a salesperson for a radio station called 54 Rock that was doing advertising with the restaurant. He was kind and witty, and we started chatting. I mentioned that I had been attending journalism school and was taking a year off to figure out what I wanted to do. He suggested I come to his workplace one day and meet some people there: he knew the program director and the guy who did the news. Maybe I could shadow them and see if that was something I might like. I remember the excited feeling of butterflies when he suggested setting this up. So we agreed on a date and time when I could come into the studio and meet everyone. It was a pivotal moment in my broadcasting career.

I watched the news anchor preparing his newscasts, ripping stories off the wire and typing them out for broadcast. He also did a weather forecast and a traffic report. I went in and shadowed while he did a news update and then met the "afternoon jock," Bob Cowan. Bob was hilarious. He could've been a stand-up comedian. I loved watching him work. He was a master at multitasking: pulling music off the shelves, following the playlist, and chatting away with me . . . then suddenly, when he saw the song was coming to an end, he would just switch the mic to "on" and—without any notes in front of him—talk about what he had played, say something about the artist, and tell a funny anecdote that would just kind of come out of nowhere. I was in awe of this talent. I also couldn't believe you could have this much fun and get paid.

One day Bob asked if I wanted to come on air with him. Maybe I could do a traffic report? OHMYGOD. I got so excited and nervous—but mostly excited. The little butterflies were being stirred up. I wrote up a script of what I thought an Ottawa traffic report should sound like:

"The Queensway is jammed up at Island Park Drive! Stay away from Bronson and Bank Street, people!" I sat next to him, put on the big headphones with the mic that flashed ON-AIR, and then Bob introduced me:

"And now with a traffic report, here's some girl we found hanging out in front of the 54 Rock studios. Janice Dean, why does a traffic light turn red?"

"Well, Bob, if you had to change in front of everyone, you'd turn red too!" Ba-da-bum.

Hearing myself through those big headphones like I did when I was four years old reciting *Alice in Wonderland*, I felt that rush of excitement and adrenaline. And those wonderful butterflies. I was hooked.

It is also worth noting that Bob never, ever hit on me or asked me out. He was a perfect gentleman and truly just wanted to help me get into the business. As you may have heard, this industry can be a little sketchy when it comes to harassment and being inappropriate, but Bob was never that guy. He was just a good person. And funny as hell.

I went into the radio station a few times a week and became a bit of a Bob sidekick on the air. I never got paid—it just kind of happened. But I was able to make some cassette tapes of our exchanges, which to me was worth more than a paycheck.

Meanwhile, I was still keeping in touch with California Tom, who I still considered a boyfriend even though he had told me on many occasions it was impossible to maintain our relationship long distance. We talked on the phone and wrote to each other. (Well, I think I wrote him letters and he wrote back once.) He knew I had quit school and was taking the year off to "find myself." I was excited to tell him about my little part-time sidekick role I was enjoying at the rock station. He used to tell me about a morning show he would listen to being stuck in LA traffic with the legendary hosts Mark Thompson and Brian Phelps. He taped some of their stuff so I could listen to it.

Since I wanted to take some time off from my numerous jobs, I asked if I could come and see him for a couple of weeks and hang out. I had stars in my eyes—not just about Tom but about visiting Los Angeles, where dreams were supposed to come true!

Tom was an engineer and a few years older. A friend of mine had been dating his roommate, and we met at one of their parties. He moved to California just a few months after that, and he was a little more realistic with his relationship expectations. My parents liked Tom, but I'm sure they weren't thrilled about their nineteen-year-old daughter ditching school and visiting an older guy living in California. I flew out to LA and had a great time hanging out in Manhattan Beach with him. I couldn't stop talking about how I thought I wanted to be a DJ or do something in broadcasting. I listened to a lot of radio out there, trying to figure out how I could learn this for a living. When the trip was coming to an end, and I was getting sad about going back home to boring old Ottawa, Tom sat me down and brought me back to reality. He told me that I could live in California, too, someday, if I wanted to. I was talented and smart and could do something great with my life. However, quitting school and hanging out at a radio station wasn't the greatest long-term plan. He was happy I had come to visit him in LA and had fun, but this wasn't reality either. Although he liked me a lot, being my boyfriend just wasn't possible.

(Cue sad trombones.)

I was crushed. Part of me was hoping Tom would be my ticket out of Ottawa, and maybe he would ask me to stay in California with him and live happily ever after? Top that off with him being my first "boyfriend," who was now breaking up with me!

WAHHHHHHHHHHHHHHHHH!

Almost thirty years later, I am incredibly grateful to Tom. He was brutally honest with me at a time when I was floating around without a clear path. It took me a while to get over the heartache. I cried during the whole airplane ride home. The flight attendants were so sweet and assumed it was boy related. This was a big moment, though. My first real wake-up call. I looked at Tom's life and how he had worked hard and was living the dream he wanted for himself. A career and happiness weren't going to magically appear. It involved hard work, dedication, and doing something I loved. I had to figure it out.

Chapter 3

SUNSCOOPED

When I got back home to Ottawa, I started researching schools that focused on radio and television broadcasting careers. There was a college in Ottawa very close to where I lived called Algonquin with a radio and television program taught by professors and instructors who were in the business. I applied and was accepted that fall. The more I learned about the program, the more excited I got. I would be getting hands-on experience while at school: there were several television studios, a campus radio station, writers' workshops, and internships. It seemed right up my alley, and something I felt finally might prepare me for my future.

Those school years flew by. I loved what I was learning. I met incredible teachers, most of whom were working in the broadcasting community. One of my favorite professors in the college was Donna Leon. She taught television but had also worked in radio and had her own production company. When people ask who my mentors in life were, Donna is up there. She was such a role model for so many of us. I think it's important to mention here that during my time at college there were a couple of teachers at Algonquin that were sexual harassers. A few women went to Donna to complain about one of these men who used his position of power to manipulate women, including sexual favors for better grades and favoritism. Donna spent many years of her career as an advocate for these students and complained on their behalf. Nothing was ever done, and this instructor continued to have a position of power at the school and in the broadcast community. Despite enjoying her job at the college and being such a terrific influence on her students, Donna decided to leave partly because of her frustration over trying to improve the college environment. This, I might add, was over twenty years ago. I surmise that things have improved, but let the record show that my friend and mentor Donna was one of the first to raise her voice and try to help before this was even a movement. I am forever grateful for her guidance, support, and being a badass before badassery was even a thing.

When I graduated from Algonquin, we had a traditional ceremony where all the students wore their caps and gowns and got up onstage to get their diplomas. I was graduating with honors and getting a special award from the college. The teachers had to nominate one student who excelled in not just his or her chosen field of study but was also representative of several of the creative arts programs. I knew I was getting the award, as did my family. My parents both came to watch me not only get my diploma but accept the medal near the end of the ceremony. We took pictures in my yard in the morning and I remember it was a beautiful day. I had accomplished so much, and I enjoyed every moment of it.

It was a long ceremony—I remember that. Hey, it takes a long time to call a couple hundred students onto the stage to shake hands and get their official document of educational achievement. I still had my special award coming up. I was sitting in my seat waiting for the announcement, when all of a sudden one of my classmates tugged my arm and pointed to my father, who was trying to get my attention at the end of the aisle. I couldn't really get up, but I was close enough to him that he could lean over a few students to give me one of the biggest disappointments of my life. He had a fifty-dollar bill in his hand and motioned to me to grab it. I wasn't registering what he was doing, and all I could think of was how weird it was that he was giving me money. He looked like he had to use the restroom; he was jumpy. And then he mouthed the words "I have to go. I have to go take care of something. Go have a nice lunch. Good job, Pookie." And then he left.

I tried not to cry. I was so pissed off, upset, mortified, embarrassed. I wanted to rip the fifty-dollar bill up into a million pieces. My mom ended up leaving with my father because she didn't really know what else to do; she was just as shocked as I was that he all of a sudden had to leave. I sat through the rest of the ceremony completely crushed. When my name was called to go up and get my medal, I remember just not really caring. I smiled and shook the college director's hand. I saw Donna Leon, my teacher, friend, mentor, and one of the professors who had nominated me for the award. She was grinning and clapping wildly for me. I don't remember much of the ceremony other than that, except when Donna saw me afterward, she asked where my parents were. I told her they had to leave, but my dad gave me fifty bucks for lunch. Would she like to join me? God bless my friend Donna. She did have lunch with me at the National Arts Centre café overlooking the Rideau Canal. I'm not sure what we talked about. She knew I was upset, and I'm sure she had many other things to do that day, but she made time for me. And told me she believed in me—that she was proud of me. I was and am so grateful for her that day, even twenty-five years later.

I asked my mom why she had left with my dad—why she couldn't stay to see me get the award. She was very remorseful; she didn't have time to really think about it and just felt she had to go with my dad. He said it was something work related that he had to take care of and that he had to leave immediately, but he never told us what it was. I'm sure if she could do it over, she would've gotten a ride with someone else or taken a taxi. I do remember she apologized. I don't believe my dad ever did. But he knew I was mad and I told him I would never forgive him.

For some reason, this is one of the toughest stories to write about, probably because I have kids now. But there was a lesson here for me later on in life. I have always said to my husband we will *never* miss a play, recital, ceremony, or important assembly for our kids. I believe that kind of stuff is so important. I will take the day off or leave early from work if I have to. Sean and I will line up outside of their school ahead of time so we can get the best seats. And every time I see my kids perform or go onstage at school, they always—*always*— look around in the audience for my husband and me. To see if we are there to watch them. And we are always there. Waving, smiling, and cheering them on. Because that's what matters.

Another one of my instructors and mentors who helped me during and after college was Mike Giunta. Mike is one of the most famous broadcast voices in Canada. He started off as a radio DJ but is also a well-known announcer. He's one of the rare talents who can broadcast in French and English at the same time. He taught one of the radio courses and recommended me for a position that changed my life.

Mike knew of a job opening at the radio station he worked at as a music director. The community events reporter at the classic rock station CHEZ (pronounced *shay*) 106 was taking maternity leave. Her beat was called the "Sunscoop" and the job was to venture around

Ottawa, attending various events and reporting live. Mike told me to come in and meet with the program director, Steve Colwill, and the promotions manager, Dave Schutte. I went in and got the job. I was thrilled! I would work on the weekends, type up a Sunscoop script of all the events I was going to report from, and do a weekly telephone recording, so you could call in and find out all the fun activities happening around the Ottawa area for your family to take part in. I wore a Sunscoop logo T-shirt and long shorts every weekend and would call in by remote from the Sunscoop CHEZ 106 Jeep at every teddy bear picnic, boat show, ice cream festival, and parade that was happening. This was the start of a delightful career in radio, one that I never imagined would take me on such an exciting journey.

Once I started at CHEZ, I wanted to learn and do more. Because I had volunteered at 54 Rock the year before and had done on-air stuff with Bob, I thought I might like to try being an on-air announcer, a DJ, or "jock" as it was called back then. I wasn't familiar with a lot of the music they played, but I was an eager student. I asked the program director if I could come in on the weekends and shadow the person on the air. Everyone was kind and helpful, and I was enjoying this potential new career.

After the summer was over, the woman I was filling in for decided to stay home for a little longer after having her baby. In addition to being the summer Sunscoop reporter, she was also the full-time on-air traffic reporter in the morning and afternoon. They needed to fill that position, so I asked if I could apply. I got the job and ended up doing that for a few years, driving around town in a big black CHEZ 106 traffic van and reporting live. Then I asked if I could try being a DJ. Listening to the station, I was familiarizing myself with the format and how to be an announcer. I bought many books on rock and roll, subscribed to *Rolling Stone* magazine, and started doing overnight and weekend shifts. I would prepare in advance, printing out my song list and writing out my "teases" before the commercial breaks. For example, if I had a Led Zeppelin song coming up, I would come up with a clever way to keep people listening during the commercials. Like this:

"Classic rock, CHEZ 106. That was Van Halen's 'Finish What Ya Started,' off the album *OU812*. Van Halen will be playing at Lansdowne park next month, and you can win tickets to that show next hour with me, Janice Dean, so keep it tuned right here, and when you hear the cue to call, be the sixth caller to win. You may even get the chance to go backstage with the band; I'll make sure you get all the details in just a few minutes. Coming up: we've got music from David Bowie, Bryan Adams, and a band whose name came from a band member of the Who when he heard Jimmy Page was looking for a group after leaving the Yardbirds. Want a hint? He said that band would go down like 'a lead balloon.' I'll have that story and some music next!"

And here's the backstory: According to *Rolling Stone* magazine, Keith Moon and John Entwistle, drummer and bassist of the Who, respectively, were recording a song with Jimmy Page, John Paul Jones, and Jeff Beck. The song came out so well, they talked about forming a new band. Keith Moon apparently joked the band would go down like a lead balloon. Jimmy Page remembered the conversation a few years later when he created Zeppelin. Over the decades, the story still hasn't been confirmed. John Entwistle always claimed he made the lead balloon joke, but it was likely Keith Moon who had the quick quip that created the name.

I told this particular story after the commercial break and right before a kickass Zeppelin song. Also worth mentioning: the art of "hitting the post." This is how many seconds an announcer has after playing the start of the song to talk up to the moment where the lead singer starts singing, so during that time, you share a little nugget about the song or even a quick weather forecast. Many DJs loved to perfect the art of hitting the post, while listeners would call in and complain that we were ruining the song by rambling on over the music. A friend mentioned to me recently that it was because people liked to record music back then and hearing the announcer talking over it was infuriating.

I loved being a "classic rock jock." It was truly one of the best jobs of my life. I was in my early twenties, playing awesome songs, and telling stories about rock and roll. I learned so much about music, to this day I can hear an opening riff and tell you the name of the artist or band and the song with only about two seconds of music. Try me. I'm that good.

Not only did I get to work at a cool rock station, but I got to meet some amazing rock gods. When I met Peter Frampton for the first time, I'm pretty sure I embarrassed him because I asked him to sign my poster "Dear Janice, here's to another 10 years in your bedroom!"—alluding to the fact that I had a *Frampton Comes Alive!* poster in my room, and this one would guarantee another decade on my wall. I have a picture of him with an incredulous look on his face as I'm grinning from ear to ear with my request.

I never actually met Rod Stewart, but he was playing an outdoor venue in Ottawa during the summer, and we were broadcasting live from Lansdowne Park—the home of the Ottawa Rough Riders for all of you Canadian Football League historians. My promotions manager Dave told me that Rod was going to do a sound check, and we could sneak in to hear him. We sat close to the stage and were the only ones there watching him besides the sound crew. He pointed at me and asked me my name. I looked around to make sure he was speaking to me.

"Yeah—you, love!" he replied.

I shouted, "Janice!"

He said, "Janice, this song is for you . . . ," and he began to sing "Have I told you lately . . ."

Swoon.

Mike Reno from Loverboy was funny. I met him a few times and introduced the band onstage at a Canada Day concert one year. (They are from Calgary, Alberta—you would recognize their hit singles "Turn Me Loose" and "Working for the Weekend.") When I was at the microphone talking about the band and getting the crowd excited, Mike came out from stage left, grabbed a mic, and yelled, "WHO KNEW BROOKE SHIELDS WOULD BE HERE TO IN-TRODUCE US!" I turned five shades of red and forgot the rest of what I was going to say, but he and I went back and forth onstage for a few moments before I finally introduced the band and they rocked the Canada Day stage at Major's Hill Park. Back in those days, I was a little more brunette than blond, and the heavy eyebrows were a thing. I already had bushy brows, but liberally used black mascara to fill them in even more.

In Canada, we had to play 30 percent Canadian content (Can-Con) on the radio. It's a Canadian Radio-television and Telecom-munications Commission (CRTC) rule that broadcasters must air a certain amount of Canadian-made content on a variety of platforms. So that meant a lot of Bryan Adams, the aforementioned Loverboy, Bachman-Turner Overdrive (BTO), Rush, the Guess Who, Neil Young, the Band, Steppenwolf . . . Let me use this opportunity to confess that sometimes I didn't play all the required homegrown mu-sic. I may have skipped over a few Bruce Cockburn songs from time to time. Sorry, Canada.

One of my favorite "meet-and-greet" rock bands was Aerosmith. It was in 1993, during their Get a Grip Tour. I interviewed two of the band members, Tom Hamilton and Joey Kramer, while we were broadcasting once again at Lansdowne Park. I was a little disappointed that Steven Tyler and Joe Perry didn't come, but the interview went well despite their absence. My promotions manager told me we could get backstage that afternoon before the sound check to meet the band. I wrapped up my interview and headed inside the stadium. There were probably about fifty people from different radio stations in the room, excited to meet one of the biggest rock groups of all time. I was standing in one corner with my colleagues from CHEZ. We were told before the band came in not to ask for one-on-one pictures with any of the guys. Instead, we were given numbers for a group picture, and when we were called, we could go up with our gang to take a photo from a professional photographer who would then mail us the pictures. Several minutes later the band walked in. Tom and Joey, whom I had interviewed earlier, came in first with some of their PR people. Then Steven Tyler and Joe Perry sauntered in. Steven scanned the room, waved at everyone, and thanked all of us for coming, but for some reason, as soon as he saw me, he made a beeline in my direction.

Holy crap.

Was he coming over my way? I remember the butterflies I had, but I thought he was coming over to talk to someone else in my group. He walked right up to me, grabbed my hand, and said:

"Hi. What's your name, beautiful?"

Ummmmmmmmmm . . . what's my name . . . what's my name? Trying to remember my name . . .

"I'm Janice Dean."

"And what's Janice Dean doing here today?"

"Well, I am a DJ for CHEZ 106—and I just interviewed your bandmates for my show. But you and Joe failed to show up."

"Hmmm . . . how did that happen? They never told me a beautiful young lady such as yourself would want to interview me. A failure on their part."

"Well, I can set things up for something later if you're interested."

"Definitely. Interested."

Just then some PR people came over and whisked Mr. Tyler away and brought him over to talk to some concert promoters and a few other people who looked more important than I did. I also noticed some barely dressed women with hair teased higher than mine with a lot of makeup on in a corner shooting daggers from their eyes toward me. I asked my program director if we could set up an interview with Steven if he would make good on his promise . . .

A few minutes later it was time for pictures with the band. I was number four and knew it would take a while to get to me. Group number one was called, and they were getting into position with the band. Steven Tyler called out:

"Where's Janice Dean?

"Janice Dean, where are you? Come here, Janice Dean!"

He was looking over at me. When Steve Tyler asks where you are and to come over, you probably should head over. So I did, and he pulled me right next to him.

"This is where you belong," he said smiling.

So, for all the group pictures, I'm standing right next to Steven Tyler with his arm securely around my waist. He asked me what I was doing after this little meet and greet, and I told him I had to get back to my job.

Truthfully, I was incredibly nervous. I was twenty-three years old and wasn't sure how to play this. He then asked me if I was going to the show that night—and he'd love to have me there. I said "Sure," and he told me he would have someone take care of me and make sure I had a good place to watch from. After the group photos were taken, I made a bold move and asked if I could have a picture taken with just him, even though we were told beforehand this would never happen. He said "Absolutely" and got the photographer to take a few snapshots of us. He told me he would sign it and send it over to the radio station.

"You are a beautiful girl, Janice Dean," he said.

I asked him if we could do an interview at some point and he may have said: "I'll give you way more than that!"

Ahhhhh . . . to be twenty-three again.

I never did go to the concert. I had to work that afternoon, and thankfully his people never got in touch with my people. But I did get the picture of us together a few weeks later. It was signed at the back: "Wet kisses, Steven Tyler."

I was thrilled. Then I heard it wasn't his signature. Someone else had signed it. I was so disappointed.

But, as luck would have it, a few years ago, I was on *Fox & Friends* talking about how I had met Steven Tyler back in my twenties and that I had a picture of him that I would love to have signed one day. I received a tweet a few hours later from someone who knew him and his PR people. He gave me an address and told me to send the picture, and he would make sure to get it signed for me—on the front, for real. I now have it displayed proudly in my office. It says:

"Janice, This time a full frontal. Love and kisses, Steven Tyler."

Twenty-five years later.

Looking back, if I did have the chance to go and see the show, hang out backstage, and party with Mr. Tyler, would I do it?

I've thought about it. A lot. I think I could write a whole movie script about it. I would still have to say no. I'd be too nervous. Even though I'm sure it would've been a whole lot of fun, and an even better story for this book!

I talk about my radio days with such fondness. It's funny, but I still have anxiety dreams about being in the studio with a record ending and I don't have another song to play—and the records have mysteriously disappeared . . .

The other recurring dreams I have are turning on the microphone to talk and I don't have anything to say. Or, I've forgotten to put my commercials into the "cart machine" (a little console where we put cartridges in with thirty- or sixty-second commercials on them). And because there's nothing to play, or "toss" to, I have to talk until I figure out what to do next, while trying to avoid "dead air" (translation: hearing nothing on the radio, which to a DJ is the eighth deadly sin). Nowadays everything is automated and on a computer, so there's less chance of dead air or not having songs or commercials to play. Even live jocks are a rarity. A lot of times you'll hear prerecorded intros and outros after songs before commercials. When I started out, we were still playing records, mixing them ourselves on turntables, and we could smoke cigarettes in the studio. Yes, I was a smoker for a few years! We also used to "cut" our own tape as well—meaning we would record something on reel to reel, and if we had to edit, we would use a razor blade and tape to splice it together after taking out whatever needed to be edited.

When we needed an extra-long bathroom or smoke break, we always knew the longer songs to play—some of those included:

Iron Butterfly, "In-A-Gadda-Da-Vida," at 17 minutes and 5 seconds
Rush, "2112," at 20 minutes and 33 seconds
Pink Floyd, "Shine On You Crazy Diamond," at 26 minutes
Elton John, "Funeral for a Friend," at 11 minutes and 7 seconds

These were songs on our playlist, but if you really wanted to get crazy, the Allman Brothers' "Mountain Jam" is 33 minutes and 41 seconds. You could get away with this if you were doing an overnight shift.

So life as a classic rock DJ in my early to midtwenties was pretty damn awesome. Near the end of my days at CHEZ, I was a cohost on the morning show—the only female among five men: Jeff Winter; Jim Hurcomb; Trigger Brown; Joe Cummings, who did sports; and Craig Steenburgh, who did news. I took over at 9:00 a.m. and did two hours of middays. I was also reporting, and occasionally I would do news anchoring. I wanted to learn everything, and that is another thing I sometimes tell young students wanting to get into the world of broadcasting: learn as much as you can, doing everything you possibly can.

Another fun thing to add here:

Back home in Canada, our version of MTV was called MuchMusic. The studios were in Toronto, and one of the biggest VJs (video jockeys) on Much was a handsome fella named J. D. Roberts. He had long, flowing '80s hair just like the rock stars he interviewed. Every girl my age had a crush on J. D. Roberts. When I was at CHEZ, someone had told me Much was looking for more female VJs for their channel. I sent in a VHS tape of some of the various television hosting jobs I did with the rock station. I got a callback from Denise Donlon, who was one of the big VIPs with Much. She told me she liked my tape but she needed to see more—could I do something a little more like reporting?—on scene at a rock club as a backdrop? I couldn't believe I got a callback. I was so excited.

My imagination was running wild: What if I got the job and J. D. Roberts and I fell in love and we got married and had little VJ babies?! I wanted this audition tape to look fantastic. I told my promotions manager, Dave, and he called one of his buddies who was a well-known camera operator and director who made music videos. We went out to Barrymore's, a live music club in Ottawa, and got a band to shoot a package with me. I wore my best overall jean dress with a mint-green turtleneck and some white canvas combat boots. I styled my naturally curly hair to smooth and VJ-like. We then edited the footage at a fancy production studio. I couriered my fabulous VJ demo to Denise and waited for the callback. When I didn't get a call a week later, I was a little depressed. I left a few voice mails for Denise and kept persisting. Finally, I got through one afternoon. She sounded a little annoyed but took my call.

"Hi, Janice. Yes, I got your tape. It wasn't really what I asked for. I wanted something a little less polished, to be honest. That demo you sent me looked too 'produced.' We want edgy here, like you're just kind of winging it. But thanks. Good luck!"

I was crushed. My dream of Janice Dean with J. D. Roberts was over.

Years later I was watching CBS news in Houston, and I did a double take. Someone who looked like J. D. Roberts was doing the news. In a suit. With a haircut. Wait a minute . . . THAT'S J. D. ROBERTS! Instead of introducing Def Leppard in a leather jacket in tight jeans, J. D. Roberts was now John Roberts reporting from the White House! Holy moly. My '80s crush was now doing big-time news.

Flash forward a few more years, and John Roberts was now being hired by FOX NEWS. OMG.

I eventually told him in person about my MuchMusic "almost hired" story with the "too-polished" demo tape. He laughed and said, "What was she thinking? You would've been great at MuchMusic!"

Ahhhhh, yes. Dreaming of double JDs introducing Whitesnake videos with matching '80s hairdos. I still get a little fangirl when I see John on television. I told my J. D. Roberts story a few years ago on the *Fox & Friends* "After the Show Show"—the five to ten extra minutes we air on the Internet—and the producers said they wanted to bring John Roberts on the curvy couch so I could share this story with our viewers. John was busy that week, so it never happened. But I'm always ready for the JD[2] reunion if and when it does happen.

Chapter 4

HOUSTON, WE HAVE A
PROBLEM

I started doing a little more television in addition to my full-time radio job back in Ottawa. Every year we had a telethon to benefit the Children's Hospital of Eastern Ontario. I was asked to host a couple of hours with a local news anchor from CBC TV. I had a blast doing it, and afterward I heard from the news director at the television station. He asked if I would be interested in doing fill-in weather for their national weather anchor, Ian Black. My first reaction was to say no, since I had never really done weather other than reading the "rip-and-read" Environment Canada forecast off the news wires.

I consulted with a few of my friends in the broadcast world, including my friend and former professor Donna Leon (who also worked part-time for CBC radio), and they all said I should do it. It would be great visibility, experience, and a boost for the radio station. So I went in and did a few days with Ian, and he trained me on the weather graphics, showing me how to draw cold fronts and areas of high and low pressure. I remember it being overwhelming, and I felt a little out of my comfort zone, but I wanted to do a good job and not back down. I drove to the studio after my morning radio shift and sat with Ian, took notes, and practiced. I'd love to say the experience was "mostly sunny," but it was a little cloudy that first week. Creating the graphics took me quite a while, since there was a whole process of getting it to animate and save in a complicated, rudimentary computer program. For me, this took much of the day to make sure I did it right. Then I stayed and did the 6:00 p.m. and 11:00 p.m. broadcasts. I taped my reports on VHS at home so that I could watch them afterward. I was doing this job in addition to my early mornings at CHEZ, so I was exhausted by the end of the week. Overall, I felt I did a pretty good job for someone who had never done weather before.

During this time, I was seriously dating a boy, also named Ian, who had just gotten a job in Houston. (Yes, a pattern of boyfriends who move to the US is duly noted.) We had a long-distance relationship for a few months, and we were planning on me eventually moving there. I sent out tapes and résumés to Houston radio stations and went to visit him every other weekend. My head was not in my job at CHEZ anymore. I felt like my wheels were stuck. The work was fine, but I wanted more adventure in my life. I always felt I needed more than my hometown could offer. When I met Ian, he told me he was looking to get out of Ottawa, so I decided this was something I wanted in my life as well.

Before I could second-guess my decision about leaving, I was laid off my job at the radio station in a series of cost-cutting measures. I was sad and depressed by this but figured it was a sign that it was time to pack my bags and get out of Dodge. As luck or fate would have it, just a few days after I was let go from my job in Ottawa,

Houston was calling and I was offered a radio gig. It seemed like the universe was telling me I was supposed to move there and Ian and I were meant to be together. I loved his family. His sister Patty and I were friends and had gone to high school together.

It was 1998, I was twenty-eight years old and excited to start my brand-new life with my boyfriend in a big American city. Then, all of a sudden, my dad left. I couldn't understand why he was bugging me to not break the lease on my apartment. He hinted that maybe he would take the lease over for me. I asked him point-blank: "What about Mom? Have you talked about this with her?" He just told me it would be nice to have another place so close to where he was working downtown. I thought it was weird, so I pushed back and said no. Besides, how was he going to pay for the apartment with the mortgage as well? My dad had a lot of money troubles. We later found out he was tens of thousands of dollars in debt. My mom told me after he left that she was grateful she had her little savings put away, because my dad had used most of their retirement money.

My mom was at work one day, and Dad stayed home and cleaned out as much stuff as he could, piled it into his car, and left. She called me and told me that he was gone. And that was it. He just pulled out of the driveway without a note or a phone call. He later left a message on the answering machine that he wanted a divorce.

My mom wasn't in good shape for many months after this. At the same time, I was moving to Houston to start my life with Ian, so I wasn't there to help her through it. I knew their marriage wasn't perfect, that my dad was very difficult to live with, but I never thought he would just up and leave. I didn't handle it very well. I just wanted to get the hell out of Ottawa. Now more than ever. Running away from everything sounded right up my alley. Selfishly, I thought their marriage wasn't my problem to solve.

I am grateful to my brother, Craig, who took the lion's share of helping Mom get through this painful, heartbreaking, devastating time. My way to deal with it was to leave. None of us talk about it very much, but Mom got through it, and in many ways, she is stronger and happier than when she was married to my dad. I wish they had separated sooner so that she could've maybe met someone else or had a happier life. She has a good support group of friends, and she is incredibly close with her siblings. I'm grateful to all of them for being there to help her through it when I wasn't.

My mom is the strongest person I know. And I don't say it often enough, but I'm proud of her.

I left Ottawa and moved to Houston with two big duffel bags, and that was it. I gave away all my furniture and left some boxes in storage.

I thought everything was going my way, but it turned out to be one of the darkest periods of my life.

I was hired at a company called Metro Networks in Houston that provided news, weather, and traffic to various radio stations. I did all of the above and met some great people. I also was doing some television as a side job here and there to keep my options open.

Meanwhile, Ian and I were barely seeing each other. Our schedules were completely different: he liked to go out at night, and I had to get up at 2:00 in the morning. We were literally passing each other as he was coming home and I was going to the radio station. There were a lot of arguments and tears. We were growing apart, and I felt like I maybe rushed our relationship. We both knew this wasn't going to work out, and we broke up. I moved in with a girlfriend named Tracy who had a spare room in her apartment.

I lived with her for a few months and then decided it was time to move into my own place. I found a one-bedroom apartment in the same complex on the ground level. I was starting to feel like my life was getting back to normal. I was promoted to a new job, as a morning show cohost on an oldies station. I was loving the work, earning a good paycheck, and becoming a little more social again after another failed relationship.

If you've ever visited Houston, you know what a rarity cool nights and fresh air can be. We were living in a constant state of air-conditioning from our apartments to our cars to the office. Fall and winter could bring a few days of relief from the AC when we could open the windows and let fresh air in. Normally I would open the windows up during the day, closing and locking them at night, but one night I forgot to.

I came home from dinner with friends, washed my face, brushed my teeth, and put my hair up.

I have never owned fancy pajamas. And I am always cold. I layer up when I go to bed with flannel men's pajama bottoms or sweatpants. I usually wear a big T-shirt and a sweatshirt on top of that. It's all about comfort and warmth when I'm relaxing at home and going to bed.

It was the weekend. I was working the morning shift during the week, so after dinner and a few drinks I was exhausted. It didn't take long to fall asleep.

The next thing I knew, something was poking me forcefully in the shoulder. I opened my eyes and tried to register what was happening. I tried to focus. In front of me was a man wearing a red bandana over his mouth and a dark hoodie with a knife in his hand. I couldn't see his face. He was pushing my arm with his other hand to wake me up.

I was still disoriented and didn't know where I was. Then it registered: this person was a stranger. He was in my bedroom, ten inches away from my face, with a knife.

This sounds crazy, but my first instinct was to be calm and say hello to him.

"Hi," I said. "Can I help you?"

His voice was muffled as he spoke to me through the bandana. He motioned to me with the knife and told me, "Take them off."

"Take what off?"

"Take off your clothes."

My heart started to race faster, and I started to panic. My mouth went dry. But for some reason I was incredibly calm—and wide-awake. I remember trying to take a mental picture of him in my mind in case I needed to identify him at some point. But he was wearing a hood on his head and a bandana on his face. And it was dark.

He told me again to take off my clothes. He showed me the knife again. I started to take off my sweatshirt; since I had a T-shirt on underneath, I thought maybe that could buy me some time to think about what I was going to do next. He told me no and motioned to my flannel pants, indicating that I should take those off first. I started taking them off. Slowly. As I was doing this, I started talking to him. Calmly.

I tried to convince him that I had valuable things. To distract him from sexually assaulting me, raping me, or killing me.

"I have lots of jewelry. I have a Gucci watch. I have a gold ring. I have money. You can have all of it. I have a new car too. I'll give you everything."

It was the only thing I could think of doing. I didn't try to fight him or punch him or scream. I just talked to him like I was having a conversation with someone I had just met. I tried to forget that this bad person had somehow gotten into my apartment and was probably going to do terrible things to me. I just had to take it moment by moment.

Then he told me to take off my sweatshirt. Then to lie down. While doing this, I kept listing all the jewelry I had that I could give him. A new watch, a gold ring, diamond earrings . . .

In reality, most of my jewelry was fake. But I made it sound like I had hundreds of thousands of dollars to give away.

I was now lying down in just my underwear and my T-shirt. He slipped the knife under my underwear to scare me. I just lay there flat and tried not to flinch. I tried to disconnect my body from my brain. I told him to please not do this. To take everything. I'd give it all up. The keys to my brand-new car—anything. All of it. My voice was calm. I was trying to hold it together. To be steady. Strong. I pretended my body was dead.

It would seem that my steady convincing worked. Before going any further, he abruptly told me to get the jewelry. He backed up, still holding the knife, and let me get off the bed. I began to try to put my pants back on, but he raised his voice and said, "NO." I dropped my pants back onto the floor.

I walked over to the jewelry box, which was on my dresser. I think he already had a bag with him in the pocket of his hoodie because I don't remember having to get one for him. I dumped the entire contents into the cloth bag. I saw a gold claddagh ring my mom had bought me from her trip to Ireland, and it almost made me cry. But I held it together and gave him everything.

I then told him I would get some money. I kept trying to distract him somehow. My mind was racing. I had gone to the bank that day and had two hundred dollars in cash. He followed me into the living room, and I looked for my purse. It wasn't where I had left it the night before. I then saw it was open on a chair near the window. All the contents were out. I looked in my wallet and realized he had already taken the money from it. It was clear to me now, This thief had robbed me first and then decided to come wake me up in my bedroom afterward to assault me.

Oh, God, now what was I going to do?

Just then, there was a loud noise from outside. It almost sounded like a gunshot. I have no idea if it was or not, but it was enough to freak him out. He ran out of the living room and out the front door.

I remember him not having to unlock the dead bolt to race out of my apartment. Which means he planned the event that once he got through the window, he could easily escape when he needed to.

After he finally left, I ran and locked the door behind him. And then I collapsed and fell apart. The fight-or-flight adrenaline drained from my whole body.

I was shaking uncontrollably. The first thing I wanted to do was get dressed. I put on my pants and my sweatshirt. I was freezing cold. I then grabbed the phone and couldn't remember any numbers to dial. Shaking, I found my address book and called my good friends Karen and George. They told me to call the police and that they were on their way.

Finally, I started to scream.

Karen and George lived only a few minutes away, and they were there when the police came. I told them what I could remember: what the intruder looked like; what he was wearing. They searched for fingerprints and took notes. I told them about the jewelry he had taken, and the money. They told me I was lucky. One of the officers showed me that the window was open. That was how he must've gotten in.

Karen helped pack an overnight bag for me with some jeans and some T-shirts, and I stayed with her and George for a few nights. I asked her if she could call my mother to tell her what had happened. I couldn't bear to call her myself—it was too hard. I was in the other room when I heard her talking to Mom. I tried not to cry. Karen told her I was okay. I was strong and not physically hurt. They would take good care of me. I was thinking of my dad. How I wished I knew his phone number to call him. I knew I wouldn't be able to say much. I just wanted to hear his voice saying, "It's okay, Pookie. I'll come get you." Like he used to when I was younger.

I never spent another night in that apartment. I called the management and told them I was leaving. They let me break my lease.

I stayed with my ex-boyfriend Ian for a while afterward. I know he felt horrible about what had happened. Maybe he felt guilty too. We never really talked about it. He was living with his sister Patty, and despite Ian and me breaking up, we were all good friends. I needed them. They were there for me, and I didn't want to be alone.

I took time off work and saw a therapist. I had never been to one before, but I was told that maybe it would be a good idea to work through this with a professional.

When I told her my story and how my survival instinct kicked in, allowing me to stay very calm and even conversational with the thief, she told me that probably saved me from being raped or worse. A lot of these guys get worked up when women react, scream, or fight. I recently read somewhere that our instincts are our best defense from danger.

My therapist also told me the fact that I was wearing a lot of clothes was probably a deterrent. I am grateful that I am always cold and liked to sleep in ugly oversized flannel pajamas and a sweatshirt with layers underneath.

I went back to work after taking a week off and decided to tell my radio audience why I was gone so long. My cohost Mike McCarthy just let me talk about the home invasion on air without interruption. He was kind and sympathetic, and it felt good to discuss it. I also thought that maybe if I told my story it would make people check that their windows were locked before going to bed, to think about installing a security system, and maybe even have something close by to protect themselves.

I was not myself for weeks, perhaps even months. Heck, I'm still not fully recovered as I write this chapter. Back at work, I was easily irritated. It didn't take much to set me off. There was one day my program director told me he wanted me to work an extra weekend and I said absolutely not. As I started walking away, he made the mistake of grabbing my arm, and I screamed at him, "LET GO OF ME!!!"

I couldn't sleep. I was in a constant state of terror. I thought it might be time for me to leave Houston.

A few days later I was called by the police to come and try to pick out my assailant in a lineup. I brought Patty with me. I remember sitting there, watching this lineup of similarly dressed men. They all had bandanas and hoodies on. They took them off. Truthfully, as hard as I might, I couldn't recognize the man. Even though I had told myself to take a mental picture of him while the home invasion was happening, the emotional side of me wanted to erase what he looked like from my memory.

A reporter who was doing a news story on the break-ins and had interviewed me later told me that the thief had a pattern: he had done the same thing to several other women. Breaking in, stealing money, and waking them up. We were all about the same age, single, living around the same neighborhood. I was one of his first victims. After me, he started getting more aggressive and eventually raped someone. Luckily, he was identified by another victim and put in jail.

I still have survivor's guilt. Why did I get by without being physically harmed? Why was I spared the worst? Why was there a loud noise late at night that spooked the intruder into running out of my apartment? Why was I the lucky one?

I will be forever grateful to my friends Karen and George. And to Ian and Patty. I had a tight group of friends that got me through it. But I wasn't the same after that. I was a powder keg ready to blow. Anxious and moody, easily upset.

My husband, Sean, tells me that when we first started dating I told him the story right away. I felt like somehow I was damaged goods. I still panic sometimes when Sean is out working late or with his friends. There have been times when my kids have come in to wake me up because they're having a nightmare or need something and it takes me right back to that night when I was tapped on the arm and saw a stranger next to my bed with a knife. I see their sweet faces, and I am relieved it's just them needing their mama.

I often think to myself: *What if I had owned a gun?* I'm not sure I would've done anything. I wouldn't have had a chance to react quickly enough. Maybe I could've grabbed it if it was in a nightstand or a drawer near my jewelry box. Could I have saved another young woman from being robbed or raped?

I don't talk about the home invasion very much. I've dealt with it in therapy, and I talked about it on the air a couple of times in Houston and Ottawa when I eventually moved back home. An op-ed in the *New York Times* by my friend Bethany Mandel, an author and political commentator, brought up that night in a heartbeat when I read the headline:

"I Wanted to Be a Good Mom. So I Bought a Gun."

I read the story. It brought tears to my eyes. Here's how it starts:

A few months after my father left our family home for good, my mother heard me screaming in the middle of the night. It was the kind of scream that made her grab her rifle in one hand and some ammo in another.

It was a spring night and I was sleeping with my window open, which was right above my bed; I loved breathing in the fresh air. That night, in that open window, I heard the banging of a ladder, and by the time my mother made it into the room and began loading her gun, a man was about to climb in.

She said something along the lines of: "Bethany, come over here. I don't want you to get his brain matter on your face." I backed up behind her and my mother raised her gun. The would-be intruder slowly backed down the ladder.

I cried for many reasons. I cried because Bethany's dad had left her. I cried because she was just a baby, and I cried because I thought of my kids. Her mom probably saved her from something horrifying when she was just a child.

There is a lot of shouting going on in our country about guns. I think we need to be having calm, thoughtful discussions about how we protect ourselves without yelling so loudly no one hears each other.

When it comes to my kids and living in a big American city where crime is more prevalent than in the city I grew up in, I would do anything to protect them. That's why I think we need to have more honest discussions about how we can arm ourselves responsibly and safely.

It might've helped that young lady in her bottom-floor apartment who accidentally forgot to lock her window on a rare cool night in Houston, Texas.

Chapter 5

IMUS

After the home invasion in Houston, I felt unsettled; I was a nervous wreck. My relationship with Ian hadn't worked out, I had no family in Texas, and I felt like I needed to move back home to figure out what I was going to do with the rest of my life. Houston was not the place where that was going to happen. I packed up my stuff, called some of my old friends in the broadcasting business, and went back home to Canada to try and heal.

I wasn't home for long. When . . .

I got a job working at an all-news radio station in Ottawa called CFRA. What started as a part-time afternoon producer's position quickly transitioned into full-time anchoring and a radio talk show called *The Broad Perspective*, kind of like a radio version of *The View* with four female anchors talking about current events. I also anchored the news on a television morning show called *Breakfast @ the New RO*. One day my coworker Rob Snow came over to my workstation and handed me something he had printed out: a job opening he had found in one of the US radio trade magazines. It was a position in New York at a famous sports station called WFAN. The description was for a news editor and on-air personality for Don Imus. It said if you had radio and television experience along with news writing and reporting skills, this could be your lucky day! Not only was it nationally syndicated, but it was also broadcast on a cable network called MSNBC.

My friend Rob said he thought I would be perfect for it.

Don Imus? Hmm. Isn't he the "shock jock" that Howard Stern had complained about in his bestselling book and then the movie *Private Parts*? Stern hated him. I needed to do more research.

I thanked Rob for thinking I was talented enough to even apply for a job in New York City. He asked:

"What do you have to lose?"

New York. The "BIG APPLE"! This was late August, almost a year after 9/11. I had visited the city a few times with friends, and at one time my dad had leased an apartment in New York while he was working on a communications project for the National Museum of the American Indian in Lower Manhattan. I came down for a weekend to sightsee, but never in my wildest dreams did I think I could one day live there.

My career thus far checked all the boxes in the job description.

I had both radio and television experience. I didn't have a boyfriend or kids. I was mobile. Most of my boxes I had moved from Houston to Ottawa a few years back were still packed. I had just redone my VHS tape of TV experience, and a CD of all my radio announcing, reporting, and on-air skills. I attached an old modeling picture to my résumé that wasn't exactly a good representation of what I currently looked like, but what the heck. It was me—just in my early twenties and 20 pounds ago. I remember writing a handwritten note to the program director, Mark Chernoff, saying don't be fooled by the Canadian address. I was a dual citizen and had a passport and a social security number, and I was ready to move to NYC! I had this strange feeling that I might get a call . . .

A few days later Mark left a message on my answering machine saying he had gotten my package and to call him back.

Holy crap. New York City is calling! My heart started racing . . . and those excited butterflies were back. I called him back right away. He said he liked my work, it looked and sounded like I had all the qualifications, and would I be interested in coming to New York for an audition? AN AUDITION? I think I had to ask him to repeat the question. He asked me if I knew who Don Imus was and if I had heard his show. I lied and said:

"Yes, I'm a huge fan!" (While reminding myself to watch *Private Parts* again to refresh my memory about what Howard Stern thought of this guy.)

Mark told me that both he and Imus producer Bernard McGuirk would interview me first. I would need to write a news script, and if that went well, they would have me stay another day and go on the air with Imus himself. Could I come next week?

I said "YES!" before I thought about it. I didn't even ask how I was going to get there or where I was going to stay. He never offered to help with transportation or lodging. He just told me a date to be there.

I couldn't wait to tell my friend Rob the next day at work. I remember his face lighting up and him saying, "Holy shit." Then he said, "I think you're going to get that job!"

I smiled and said, "Well, at least I could say I was a contender!"

My boss at CFRA was also very excited and told me to "go for it." He knew it wasn't every day a girl from Ottawa, Canada, would be auditioning for a big-time radio personality. He also asked if I knew who Don Imus was. I told him I knew of him and saw *Private Parts* several years ago, which wasn't a shining endorsement, but how bad could the guy be? It was probably all an act. RIGHT?

The airfare to New York was outrageous, so I decided to drive there. When I look back on this time in my life, I am in awe of my carefree attitude. Of course I was going to drive myself to New York City!

I printed out the directions from Ottawa to New York from MapQuest. I booked a crappy hotel off the Grand Central Parkway near Astoria, Queens, where the radio station was.

Off I went, with a brand-new Jones New York pantsuit with the tags still on and some gas station snacks and my '80s CD hits. Even if I didn't get the job, I couldn't pass up the experience. I checked into my shady hotel and went to sleep that night telling myself that maybe if anyone was good enough for this job, it was me.

I drove to WFAN the next day. The radio station was in the Kaufman Astoria Studios, a famous movie studio in Queens that's known for filming *Goodfellas* and *Carlito's Way* as well as TV shows like *Sesame Street*. I didn't even notice that the WFAN studios were below street level and very run-down. Mark met me in the lobby, and we made our way through the maze down the elevator and into the bowels of the building.

I was introduced to a few of the newsroom people, who seemed nice and dressed in casual wear. There were sports jerseys all over the place—on the walls and on the staff. He told me a bit about the job: the woman who was leaving, Christy Musumeci, had just given them her notice and was going to MSNBC to be a news anchor. We walked into Mark's office, and I began dazzling him with my broadcasting experience. I had done both radio and morning television in Houston and in Ottawa. I told him about my hosting my show called *The Broad Perspective* and how I had written news in the past and anchored as well. He then brought in Imus's producer, Bernard McGuirk, whose first question was:

"So, have you heard of Imus, and why on earth would you want to work for him?"

I laughed nervously, and I think I said something to the effect of:

"I like new challenges and have a soft spot for grumpy old men?"

They asked me if I could come in the next day, sit with Christy, and meet the rest of the group. Imus was at his home in New Mexico, so lucky for me I wouldn't have to be in the studio with him. He would be on remote. And I would meet his cohost Charles McCord, who, if I got the job, I would be writing the news for.

I got to the radio station the next morning and spent a good amount of time driving around Astoria, looking for a spot to park (my first of thousands of expeditions in Queens in search of a parking space).

I met Christy, who was kind and helpful as she walked me through the job in the morning. She told me that, along with writing news for Charles and a business report for Imus, I was also responsible for the "scum report."

"A *what*?" I asked.

She told me it was an entertainment report, but Imus wanted it to be down and dirty on celebrities. If it was lame, he'd throw me out of the studio. Yikes. I asked what he was like. She looked at me and said:

"You've got to have a thick skin. Some days he'll think you're fine and others he'll say: 'You suck.'

"Just try to be 'one of the guys.'"

I wrote the news for Charles and tried to write this scum report thing. I looked at the entertainment wires for stories but couldn't find much. Ugh. I found a story about a bad hair day for Britney Spears.

Charles McCord was as nice as could be. *Okay, well, if he's nice, I thought, maybe that's a good indication that the "I-man" can be pleasant too?*

Bernard McGuirk, his producer, was in the other room with Lou Rufino, the board operator/engineer. Sid Rosenberg was his sports guy. Each of them was kind to me and at some point asked what a nice Canadian girl was doing in a dump like this?

It was my turn to go in and introduce myself to Imus. I went in and put my headphones on and took a deep breath. I could see Imus at his ranch in the studio monitor with his big cowboy hat before we went to air. He was cursing about something, chewing his Nicorette gum, and looking for a live commercial script to read.

Imus then went on the air talking about the fact that Christy was leaving to go to that "hideous MSNBC," and they were interviewing new people. He asked me who I was and where I was from. I gave him my name and announced that I was from Ottawa, Canada. He asked if I knew Peter Jennings, the well-known ABC news anchor. Wasn't he Canadian? Coincidentally, Peter was from my hometown, Ottawa, and I told him he got his start as a teen dance show host. I then told him I met him at a bar once.

"WHAT?"

Bernard, Lou, and Sid started to perk up. I could tell they were starting to like where I was going with this Peter-Jennings-walks-into-a-bar story . . .

"Oh, really??? What happened next?"

I said I didn't remember. I was more focused on the hockey team that was hitting on my friend. Or something like that. I used the hockey team reference a lot.

The guys laughed.

"Ever date a hockey player?"

"Well, that's a requirement if you're a Canadian female."

Anyhow, I think it went something like that. I tried to be "one of the guys," like Christy had told me.

I knew I had done okay, and it seemed like Imus was in a good mood. The guys all told me they thought it was a solid audition, but there were other, local New York women they were interviewing, so I was a "long shot."

I saw Mark Chernoff afterward, and he told me it went well, but it wasn't up to him. He'd call me and let me know—and suggested the dark horse sometimes wins the race.

I drove back to Ottawa feeling like maybe I had a chance at this thing. I went back to my other job. Many of my coworkers told me they had watched me on MSNBC and said I had fit right in.

I got a call a few days later from Mark, asking if I could come back for a second audition. They had two other women they were looking at along with me. This time they would pay for a hotel in the city for me to stay in. I asked my boss if it was okay for me to do another audition. He told me he had a feeling I'd be coming back to pack my bags for good.

On the second audition, I went in and worked a full morning shift. I wrote all of Charles's newscasts and did a scum report. I put together a business update for Imus as well. The guys were all very nice and helpful. I'm pretty sure Bernard asked me a few times:

"Are you sure you want this job?"

I don't think Imus or Bernie thought I was the best person for the job, but I think Sid and Lou liked me. I had heard Imus asked them who they thought had the best audition. He said he didn't like any of us, but Sid and Lou liked the Canadian girl. Mark Chernoff told me he would let me know who got the job before I checked out of the hotel.

That morning I walked around Manhattan after the show. I remember seeing storefronts that were still shut down a year after the terrorist attacks, but the city felt more alive than ever. It was a beautiful fall day. I started believing this could happen . . . New York City, baby!

I got the call in the midafternoon. Mark congratulated me: "Welcome to WFAN!" He told me my salary ($60,000 a year, which would've been awesome . . . in a small town in the Midwest!) and asked me when I could move there. Could I do it in two weeks? WHAT THE HECK? I had to find a place to stay. I had to move my stuff again. I didn't know a soul in New York City. But I didn't care. This was the opportunity of a lifetime. I would figure the rest of it out.

I went back home, packed my bags, and moved to New York. My friends and colleagues had a going-away party for me. I wore a Statue of Liberty costume, had some drinks, some laughs, and hugged everyone goodbye. My mom came and so did my friend and mentor Donna Leon. All my cohosts from *The Broad Perspective*, coworkers from the radio stations over the years, and some of my high school pals were there. I was touched at the big turnout. Looking back, this was a major turning point in my career and personal life. I was on top of the world.

What I didn't know is it would be the worst job I've ever experienced.

There were a handful of days where Imus would tell me I was doing a good job. Most of the days, however, he would ignore me or tell me I sucked. I never knew when he would decide to call me in to do a scum report and my stomach was constantly in knots throughout the morning. Bernard would ask if I had anything "good" for him, and sometimes he would rip front pages off the *National Enquirer* for me to use.

A simple entertainment report would not do. It had to be scandalous. I remember one day Bernie told me I *had* to report a story about a cable news host flubbing a Jennifer Lopez story. He had cut some tape of this newscaster named Shep Smith saying "blow job" instead of "curb job." (This has since then gone down as one of the top ten newscaster bloopers of all time.) It was perfect scum material.

I reported it, and everyone laughed. Little did I know the newscaster I was doing a scum report on would be someone I'd be working with a year later.

There were a few times I could do a scum report on people who came to visit Imus. Case in point: Dr. Phil.

I've met a lot of "celebrities" through the years. Some of them have been gracious; others couldn't wait to get the interview or the event out of the way and get back into their self-important bubble away from gen pop. Working as a DJ over the years, I've done pretty much every music format: classic rock, country, smooth jazz, top forty, oldies, easy listening . . . I would say, as a general rule, country music musicians are the nicest to deal with. They seem more humble and thankful for their success, and don't forget their roots and where they came from. Examples would be Tim McGraw, Brad Paisley, Keith Urban, Travis Tritt. One of my favorite ladies of country music, Dolly Parton, is also on this list, although I've never met her in person; I've just talked to her through the magic of TV satellite interviews. When it comes to not-so-nice celebrities, you can see these snobby, entitled stars coming a mile away with their attitudes and airs of importance. However, I would say, for all the divas, I've met way more down-to-earth "celebs" to make up for their holier-than-thou counterparts.

It's a little disappointing meeting people you looked up to or enjoyed watching or listening to growing up. Dr. Phil is one of them. I was a big fan of Oprah Winfrey's in my teens and twenties. I watched her show religiously every weekday at 4:00 p.m. when I would come home from school. Dr. Phil McGraw was a regular on her show after he helped her win the infamous Amarillo, Texas, beef lawsuit trial. He had just launched his new show, *Dr. Phil*, and was promoting it. When I saw he was on the calendar to come in and be on *Imus*, I was so excited. I asked my program director, Mark, if I could greet Dr. Phil in the lobby when he came in for his interview. I couldn't wait to tell him how much I enjoyed him and his expertise, his down-to-earth way of telling people they had major problems.

Little did I realize, Dr. Phil seemingly had his own issues.

As soon as he walked in through the door of Kaufman Astoria Studios, you could tell he was not the fella you see before and after commercial breaks. He had an entourage of people with him as I walked up and introduced myself.

"Hello, Dr. Phil!" I said with excitement. "Welcome to the show! I'm Janice Dean with *Imus in the Morning*."

He didn't even look at me. He just motioned for his "people" to talk to me.

My heart sank. Oh, but it gets better . . . or worse (lol).

We all rode the elevator together, with Dr. Phil still ignoring me all the way. His entourage wasn't exactly being chatty either. I still tried to be a goodwill ambassador.

"Here we are . . . ," I announced when we got down to the basement of WFAN studios. "Can I get you—"

Before I could finish my "Can I get you anything? Coffee or water?" they all brushed past me quickly and walked by the front desk. I trailed behind them. Bernie greeted Dr. Phil, and he all of a sudden came to life like the guy I saw on TV with his southern drawl and wide, toothy (fake) smile: "How y'all doing?" Bernard took them into the studio to meet Charles. I think Imus was at the ranch at the time, because I normally wouldn't be so bold as to go into the studio unannounced.

My "mostly sunny" attitude continued to give Dr. Phil the benefit of the doubt: Maybe he was just having a bad day? But when Charles McCord asked to take a picture with Dr. Phil, he motioned for Bernie to get in as well:

"Come on over, boys. Too bad the I-man ain't here!"

They all ignored me as I stood there, even though I was hoping to sneak into the photo. Just as I was making my way over to be included with "the boys," Dr. Phil put his arms around Bernie and Charles and said:

"Make sure you post this picture in your offices. When the ladies see us all together like this, you all are sure to get laid . . . and you can thank me later." Guffaw, guffaw.

What a dick was all I could think of. I walked out of the studio. And then told everyone after that about my "sure to get laid" Dr. Phil story.

I was at a taping of Dr. Phil in LA a few years ago and had the chance to meet him again. I avoided him.

One celebrity who surpassed my expectations was Patrick Swayze. Oh, yes, I saw *Dirty Dancing* many, many, many times. It's one of those films that I can't stop watching if I stumble on it while channel surfing.

I was seventeen when that movie came out and was mesmerized by everything about the bad-boy dance instructor with a heart of gold, Johnny. I remember seeing that movie in the theater and dreaming about being Baby in a corner with this hunky actor. Then there was the classic "so-bad-it-was-great" movie *Road House*, with the famous line "Pain don't hurt!" which I have printed on a T-shirt. And then came *Ghost*, with that Demi Moore pottery scene. If you were a girl growing up in the '80s or early '90s, you didn't have a pulse if you didn't think Patrick Swayze was a dreamboat. We were all crushed to hear he was married—but then, as you got older and saw that he was still married to his wife, Lisa, for decades, you would conclude that he seemed like a dedicated husband who didn't cheat, which is bonus points for us who had crushes on him in our teens and twenties.

I met Patrick Swayze when I was living in Houston in 2000. He was there for a fund-raiser in Wharton, Texas, just outside of the city. Patrick was one of Houston's most famous hometown boys, having been born there, and always proud of his Bayou City heritage. I had heard he was in town and just wanted to meet him. I found out where he was going to be through some media connections and hung out with the press. When he arrived, he did impromptu interviews and talked with everyone. I was just there with a girlfriend—and my little Canon camera, hoping for a picture. He came over and chatted with me—smiling that beautiful smile. He asked where I was from—how I liked living in Houston—how he loved coming back. He was happy to take a picture with me, and I like to tell myself that if he didn't have other things to do, he might've stayed and chatted a little longer.

The world was heartbroken when we heard he was diagnosed with pancreatic cancer and when he passed away far too soon in 2009. When I was looking through pictures to include in this book, I saw our photo together and smiled. It took me right back to the moment, and reminded me it only takes a few seconds to make an impression on someone. Patrick Swayze was the real deal. Both Dr. Phil and Imus could learn a thing or two . . .

I learned quickly never to say hello or acknowledge Imus when he walked in. You would be at risk of being attacked or yelled at. Everyone was on alert when he was in the building. He also carried around a gun with him and let everyone know he had it on him at all times.

One morning he came out of the on-air studio, stopped, and pointed his gun a few feet away from the back of the traffic reporter's head. And snickered to himself. I saw it happening. I was just a desk away from hers.

Sometimes he would take the bullets out in front of us one by one and say, "This one could be for Bernie. This one could be for Lou, and JANICE . . ."

Yes, he named the bullets from his gun after us. How sweet.

There was one time we had a young intern with us. He was so excited to be there and couldn't wait to meet Imus. One of the guys took him aside and told him not to look at or talk to the angry man in the cowboy hat when he came into the newsroom, especially if Imus didn't know who he was. The intern didn't take the advice, though, because as soon as the mean urban cowboy walked in, the poor guy stared at him. Imus knew right away the kid was in awe, and yelled, "Stop looking at me, you fucking moron. I'll shoot that fucking beanie off your head so fast, it'll make your head spin." The intern, by the way, was Jewish. I was mortified. So was he. I was praying that this young student from Fordham University would go and tell his parents about being threatened by this washed-up radio jock with a Glock and maybe Imus would get fired.

That of course never happened.

Did I ever think he was going to shoot us? I didn't think so, and thankfully we're all still here. We would nervously laugh about it with each other in the hallway. I think a lot of us had Stockholm syndrome. This was just our reality, and we had to deal with it. Mark Chernoff, the program director, knew. All the bosses knew. However, no one would do anything about it. He was too powerful and making WFAN and MSNBC millions of dollars.

As far as I knew, there was no HR at WFAN. Or there might've been, but I had no idea where to go. There was no one to complain to, and everyone just kind of knew this was what the workplace was like. For some reason, he seemed meaner to women. I was becoming a big target.

The guys tried to help me. They would laugh at my scum reports when Imus wouldn't. Sid, the sports guy, would come into the studio with me because we had a good rapport and would bounce off each other well. He mistreated Sid, too, and gave everyone a hard time, including Charles, but they were used to it and could let it roll off their backs. Bernard would make the joke that when Imus asked for coffee, he would make sure to make a pit stop in the bathroom to pee in the cup before pouring the coffee into it. I'm not sure Bernie would ever admit it. I wouldn't blame him if he did. None of us would.

There were times I would have a good day: I would have a great scum report and Imus would acknowledge me. However, most of the time he would call me an idiot, stupid, useless, a moron, and he would also comment on my appearance.

I had to do my own hair and makeup for this job, and let's just say I didn't look like the lady you now see on Fox News. I would put hot rollers in my short hair to give it some kind of style, but admittedly it looked like old-lady hair. And I wore pantsuits. Every. Single. Day. I always thought of the job as a radio gig. I never really thought about the fact that we were also on TV. (What's cable?) So I didn't place a lot of importance on my appearance. Put it this way: I had a make-over team from the TLC channel calling me on a weekly basis to see if they could help out. Imus and Bernie were addressing me as Mrs. Doubtfire. I went through with the makeover show before I handed in my resignation. UGH. It was all so embarrassing.

Imus and Bernard would comment on my weight. A LOT. This was a sore spot for me, because, as you know, I had been teased and bullied in school about being fat.

One day we had Denise Austin, a famous fitness trainer, on the show. Imus called me into the studio, and I could tell I was in for it. He asked me to stand up in front of the cameras while we were on the air. He then pointed out every part of my body that I needed to shape up or lose weight from. Hips, butt, thighs. All of it. "Don't you want to meet a guy? You can't find someone looking like that."

I was mortified. I remember trying to defend myself and joke:

"Well, according to my latest Weight Watchers meeting, I'm well within the guidelines for my height of being healthy."

I would drive home crying most days. I had achieved my childhood dream, but the gap between who I was on the broadcast and who I was at home would never be bigger. Listeners heard someone smart, sassy, informed, and confident. Off the air, I felt broken and alone.

In those days of turmoil, when I should've been at the top of my career, I started thinking about my dad's advice: "Do what you most love to do, and it will never feel like work."

I knew in my heart this was not what I was meant to be doing. I was thinking about Dad a lot lately. Would he be proud of me right now?

One day, in between scum reports, I started talking with one of Imus's regular guests, Bo Dietl, who was a former cop and private investigator. I asked him just for the hell of it if he could find my dad for me.

"Find your dad? You don't know where your father is? Is he a Canadian criminal or something?"

I shrugged my shoulders. Truthfully, nothing would surprise me. We thought he had been living in Nebraska for a while, but it was like he had dropped off the face of the earth.

I gave Bo the information I had, not thinking that I would hear from him, and a few days later the phone rang in the WFAN newsroom. Bo Dietl had found my father, and Dad knew it was me trying to find him.

Sid picked it up:

"Hello . . . Yes . . . Of course she's here. Hang on."

Sid walked over to me with the phone:

"Janice Dean, I got your father here on the line. He says his name is Howard?"

"WHAAAAAAAT?" I looked at him wide-eyed. "Ummm . . . can you take a message?"

Sid looked at me weird and shrugged his shoulders. "Okay . . . but you're right here beside me. Can't you talk to your dad now?"

I just shook my head and mouthed the word "NO!" I think he saw the color drain from my face and finally understood this was not a typical father-daughter call.

"Uhhh, Janice can't come to the phone right now, but can I take your phone number down, Mr. Dean?"

I told Sid afterward I hadn't talked to my dad in over five years. I couldn't just say "Hey, Dad, how's it going?" after not knowing where he was or being in touch.

I called him back when I had my composure and could catch my breath. I think I even wrote down questions to read if I got tongue-tied.

I dialed the number and he answered right away, calling me by my childhood nickname:

"Hey, Pookie. You hit the big time, eh? Working in New York with Imus? I watch you all the time."

What the hell? You watch me all the time and yet you haven't reached out to my brother, Craig, or me in years?

I didn't say this. I was thinking it, though.

He told me he was living in Nebraska with his girlfriend and gave me their phone number and address. That was about it. We hung up, and I wondered who this man was that I called my dad all these years.

I didn't speak with him on the phone again. We communicated by email. I remember I sent him a Christmas message and didn't include his now wife—whom I had never met—on the greeting. He got mad that I didn't address her, and the emails stopped.

It would be a few years before I heard from him again.

Things weren't getting better with Imus either. In fact, it was getting progressively worse. He loved to now put me on the spot, to embarrass me when I least expected it. He would sometimes put a listener on the air who wanted to go on a date with me. Then I would make up stories about how I was drinking more, drunk all the time, trying to find a man, etc. That became my schtick. They liked the desperate-woman bit.

One day he was promoting an electric toothbrush on the air and decided it would be funny if I came in and he turned on the toothbrush and I would fake an orgasm. He wanted me to moan and groan like Meg Ryan in the movie *When Harry Met Sally* at the famous Katz's Delicatessen in front of all the customers. I did it because I didn't have much of a choice. It got lots of laughs from the guys, and even Imus said, "Great job." But when I got out of work, I knew I couldn't keep doing this.

Side note: I used to love the movie *When Harry Met Sally*, and now I can't watch that famous scene without getting hives.

Now, if you didn't know me personally, and you listened to me or watched me on TV, would you know I was lonely and sad? Probably not. You might even come to the conclusion that I was connecting with the audience, quick-witted, even happy! My dreams should be coming true!

Sadly, off air, this was not the case. Happy on the outside. Terribly sad and lonely on the inside.

Chapter 6

FATE

Because I felt so disconnected in New York, I was traveling back to Ottawa every other weekend to visit friends and family to keep my sanity. One weekend I had dinner plans with my friend Lianne Laing, who was just back from her honeymoon in Hawaii with her new husband, Tony. Lianne and I had met each other when we were both working in radio in Ottawa. I wrote her an email one day because she had written a beautiful op-ed about her dad, who had tragically died from a heart attack before her wedding day. He couldn't walk her down the aisle as she had always dreamed he would, and it touched my heart because of my estranged relationship at the time with my dad. I wrote her telling her how moved I was by her piece in the *Ottawa Citizen* and how it made me realize I needed to get in touch with my father before it was too late. When I hosted *The Broad Perspective*, she was a regular panelist, and we became good friends.

Lianne and Tony got married and flew to Hawaii for their honeymoon in the fall of 2002, around the same time as I was getting the

Imus job. Near the end of their trip, they decided to go on a hike where they met a young firefighter from New York. And that's where our love story begins.

When Sean and I tell the story of how we met, he usually takes it from there. I miss some of the important details, like why exactly he couldn't surf one day and decided to do a hike instead. I asked him to take over the next few paragraphs from here, and I'll circle back with the rest of the story:

When the aftereffects of 9/11 finally eased, I took inventory of many things in my life, including some of my hobbies and interests that I had ignored for many years. Surfing was one of those marginalized pursuits, and it now became a priority. My lifetime dream was to visit Hawaii. I chose early November—the beginning of the winter surf season—to head over.

After some time there, and mixed success with the powerful Hawaiian waves on Oahu's famed north shore, almost everyone I met told me that I had to visit at least one more island before I headed back to the mainland. I picked Kauai, the Garden Island, known for its natural beauty. I packed my boards, took the quick flight, rented a car, and drove over to Princeville on the north shore.

My dreams of surfing another Hawaiian island were quickly dashed when a gigantic swell from the North Pacific, generated by intense storms near the Aleutian Islands, sent monstrous waves crashing into the north shore of Kauai. My boards stayed in their bag. I had to find something else to do in the next day and a half.

I found out not far from where I was staying was a trailhead at the beginning of the Nā Pali Coast, one of the most picturesque places on earth, and the hiking was breathtaking.

It was on the trail that I met a wonderful couple named Lianne and Tony who were on their honeymoon. We struck up a conversation. After they found out I was from New York, Lianne mentioned that a friend and

colleague had recently taken a job in New York City. We made it to the
falls together and hiked out the full four miles as a group.

At the end of the hike, we said our goodbyes in the parking lot, and when
we were pulling out, I remembered that I had one last FDNY T-shirt left
to give someone. Before the trip, I had packed around a half dozen shirts to
give to people who did me a favor or whom I connected with, or just to give
as a goodwill gesture. I sped behind their car and honked. They stopped,
and I got out and gave them my last shirt. They quickly proposed that we
have dinner together that evening. The last thing I wanted to do was crash
a couple's honeymoon, but they were both insistent. I gladly accepted.

It was during dinner that I remember Lianne bringing up her friend in
New York City again. Maybe we should meet each other—at least for a
cup of coffee—so that she (Janice) would have at least one friendly face in
the scary Big Apple. Why not? We each wrote down our information on
little scraps of paper after a wonderful evening and parted ways . . .

When Lianne got back from her honeymoon, she asked me when
I would be back in Ottawa. She was dying to tell me about her trip
AND the person she just met that I should get to know. It just so
happened I was coming home the following weekend to see my mom
and escape my abusive cowboy hat–wearing boss.

Lianne and I met for dinner. We ordered drinks right away and,
bypassing many details of her honeymoon, she began to tell me
about the New York City fireman she and Tony had met on their
hike. (She also may have mentioned how great a matchmaker she
was.) I was single. He was single. More importantly, I didn't know
anyone in New York. He might be a good person to get to know,
even if it wasn't a romantic connection.

"BUT wouldn't it be great if you did fall in LOOOOOOO-
OOOOVE???? What a story to tell your kids someday . . . ," Lianne
might've said with a twinkle in her eye.

She pulled out a worn-out piece of paper with a faded phone

number and email address on it and told me the story of how she almost lost the number in her shorts pocket when she and Tony jumped into the hot tub. They were so exhausted after the hike and dinner that they hopped in with all their clothes still on, when Lianne suddenly remembered she had Sean's information to pass on to me in her pocket! She pulled out the wet piece of paper and gently laid it out to dry so that it didn't smudge. The ink was still legible. I remember telling Lianne that meeting a man was the last thing I wanted to do just then, but I appreciated her dedication. I didn't like my job, I didn't love New York, and why on earth would I want to start a relationship with someone if I wasn't sure that was where I wanted to live? She said at the very least he could maybe introduce me to some of his friends or show me the city. What did I have to lose?

Lianne was a good pitchwoman. When I got back to New York, I emailed Sean and told him I was the crazy Canadian lady that his new hiking friends told him about and, if he wasn't too scared, would he want to meet sometime for coffee? He wrote back a day or so later, and we arranged a meeting spot after my early-morning job when he was getting off work as well from a twenty-four-hour shift. I still have the directions he sent me detailing the drive into the city from Astoria.

In our back-and-forth correspondence he also mentioned he would be wearing a dark coat and he had a lot of prematurely gray hair for someone in his early thirties, since we hadn't yet met in person.

I had never seen the Rockefeller Center Christmas Tree, so Sean took that into account and said he would look into a place near the tree. True to his word, he was standing at the corner of Third Avenue and East Fifty-First Street with his navy jacket and his shock of white hair.

"Hi. I'm Sean."

"Hi, I'm Janice."

At first glance I thought Sean was very handsome. He had a kind face with beautiful blue eyes. He was taller than me. Admittedly this has always been on a bit of a checklist when it comes to men. I'm five feet eight inches and not a small girl, so I've always felt a little better if the guy I'm with is at least twenty pounds heavier and at least two inches taller. Also, he had a fantastic voice. The Brooklyn accent was a definite bonus. It reminded me of one of my favorite films, *Saturday Night Fever*, although Sean's accent wasn't as thick as Tony Manero's and he wasn't wearing white disco pants.

Sean had wanted to take me to the Rock Center Café, next to the tree, but it wasn't open yet, it was still too early in the morning, so we decided to walk around to find another place.

We stumbled upon a diner right across the street from St. Patrick's Cathedral on West Fifty-First Street called Prime Burger. The décor hadn't been updated since at least the 1950s. It felt like we were in an episode of *Happy Days*. The slogan above the door read "The Gates of Heaven—Never Closed" due to the proximity of the famous church across the way. If I'm not mistaken, they also filmed a scene there for *Sex and the City*, which I watched religiously before moving to New York. The tables were like old school desks, and apparently regulars like Rita Hayworth, Henry Fonda, and Sammy Davis Jr. used to cram themselves into the tight booths with the swivel trays.

It was too early for burgers, so we had omelets. I gave him a *Reader's Digest* version of my move from Ottawa to Houston and back to Ottawa.

Sean has playfully told people that he remembers I talked A LOT on this first "not-a-date" breakfast. And that I had crazy, short, puffy hair. Thankfully, that also didn't scare him off.

We both agree that this was not love at first sight. I am grateful for that, to be honest. We weren't looking for a romantic relationship. I had had a string of unsuccessful boyfriends, and Sean had recently broken up with someone he had dated for several years. It was just an excellent breakfast with a kind person with a cool Brooklyn accent. Being a New York City firefighter was also incredibly attractive. They are real American heroes.

Since this was a year after the worst terror attack in United States history, it was hard not to ask if he was there that fateful day.

Knowing Sean as I do now, the 9/11 question is something that he doesn't take lightly. He will tell people he lost many of his friends that day. What he told me that morning at breakfast made my heart leap into my throat.

Sean was off duty that day, studying for the lieutenant's test. His driver's license had expired, so he woke up early to get it renewed at the DMV. He got there at 8:00 a.m. and breezed through the express line. (His driver's license with the issue date of 9/11/01 is now tucked away in a safe-deposit box.) He got home and was going to go for a run, so he turned on the television to get the forecast. That's when he saw the news of a plane crashing into the first World Trade Center tower. He lived just a few blocks from the firehouse, on Sixty-Sixth and Amsterdam, so he grabbed his keys and his cell phone and rushed over to see if he could help. Sean threw on his gear and was able to get a ride with a Red Cross truck, which dropped him off around Chambers Street. As he was walking down West Street, the second tower fell. Sean spent the whole day trying to find his brother firefighters and helping others who were injured or in shock. He walked through and breathed in the toxic ash that had settled on the city like a thick gray blanket. Afterward, he spent many weeks digging and sifting through debris to find anything he could to give to the families of those who had been lost.

Three hundred and forty-three firefighters died on September 11, but eighteen years later we've lost over 150 first responders from 9/11-related illness. Many more are sick. Sean has said he thinks he will eventually be diagnosed with a World Trade Center illness from breathing in the poisoned air in the days, weeks, and months that he looked for his friends' remains.

A few years ago, when Sean and I visited the 9/11 memorial, we walked through a dark corridor that tried to re-create some of the pictures and sounds of the area immediately after the attacks. Through the speakers, we heard what Sean explained are firefighter PASS (personal alert safety systems) alarms, which are meant to activate when a firefighter is immobile for more than thirty seconds. He told me that sound brought him back immediately to that day. When he heard all those PASS alarms go off, he knew they were all attached to dead firefighters. Dozens and dozens of them were beeping. The only sounds right after the collapses were the alarm noises.

Sean carries survivor's guilt because he was spared that day when twelve men from his firehouse were not. It's something he will live with for the rest of his life, and a feeling that still overwhelms him when the weather starts to get cooler and the school year approaches. Our kids know their dad is a fireman, but they have no idea of the profound story and history he has lived through.

Sean wears the WTC ribbon with two stars on his dress uniform, designating that he is a "Survivor" who arrived before the second collapse. There are not many living members who were awarded the two-star ribbon. That little safe-deposit box holds a lot of New York history and bravery that will eventually belong to our sons. Sean has told me on several occasions he doesn't want our boys to grow up to be firemen. I gently remind him that that's not for him to decide.

I knew that morning in December of 2002 that I had met someone special, but it wouldn't be for a few more months that it turned into something more than just friendship.

After our first breakfast together in the Prime Burger, we would hang out together once in a while. Sean would call me when there was something he thought I might be interested in coming to: an art gallery event, or if some of his buddies were playing in a band one night. Would I come and watch firemen pretend they were rock stars?

I do remember the exact night I finally got butterflies, and things shifted from friendship to romance. We met for dinner at a Belgian restaurant in the East Village that someone had recommended. We had french fries and beer and had some good laughs. It just felt easy being with him, and we had a lot of common interests. That night in my car, when I dropped him off at his apartment, we shared our first kiss. It felt both exciting and brand-new.

Maybe New York City wasn't so bad after all . . .

Just when my social life was getting so much better, that asshole Imus tried to ruin it.

Sean and I were seriously starting to date, and I had brought him to a bar to meet some of my work friends one night. Imus's driver, Brant Eaton, was there. At the time I didn't think anything of it. However, Brant was a huge gossip. He was like a giddy schoolgirl when he could report back to Imus on things he might find interesting about his staff. Janice Dean, "scum reporter" from Canada, was dating a New York City firefighter. It was gold. It also could've seriously harmed my relationship with Sean.

The devil in a cowboy hat decided to call me into my studio one day, and he had an evil grin on his face.

I grabbed my scum report stuff, thinking he wanted me to dish the celebrity dirt. He waited until the commercial break was over, and then he got Lou to turn on my microphone. I had no idea what he was up to, but he had that look in his eye that he was going to do something mean.

"So . . . what's this I hear about you dating a fireman?"

My face went red. My heart started to beat faster.

"Uhhh . . ." I couldn't think of anything witty to say to try to change the subject.

"Yeah, Brant told me you were dating a fireman named Sean. You brought him out to a bar last week. How's that working out for ya?"

I felt my throat dry up and my stomach began to churn.

My mind was racing. I didn't want this on the air. I knew right away Sean would be furious if his name was out there. He already knew how much I hated what I was doing, how they treated me. Now he was an innocent bystander being brought up by a horrible man who just wanted to embarrass me and ruin my life. None of this was good.

I quickly lied and pretended like I had no idea what he was talking about. I tried to use the old politician's excuse, "I don't remember . . . I don't recall . . . ," and then added: "I must've been drinking. Actually, I may be drunk right now!" Cue nervous laughter.

I had to tell Sean immediately afterward that his name and profession were brought up on the air. He was not pleased. We hadn't been dating that long, and I was scared this would make him rethink dating this reluctant, remorseful, and shameful scum reporter.

Sean told me in no uncertain terms he did not want his name on the radio. He never wanted his name or face anywhere near the media with all that firefighters were going through a year after 9/11.

I told him I would make sure it wouldn't happen again. Sean knew I was deeply unhappy with my job and actively searching for something else in the industry. I was crying all the time, and despite trying to hide that side of my life from him, it was creeping into our relationship.

Thankfully, when I couldn't take the Imus job anymore, I managed to get a job interview in the fall of 2003 with Roger Ailes at Fox News.

Chapter 7

ALWAYS BE NICE TO THE HAIR
AND MAKEUP PEOPLE

While I was working at *Imus in the Morning*, I was also working part-time at the local CBS station in New York as a weekend traffic reporter. I had to do something else: the Imus job was not paying enough to cover the insane amount of rent they get away with in New York. On Saturdays and Sundays, I would head into the city and do local TV. Back then I worked seven days a week. I didn't love the job, but it was supplementing my income. While I was there I met a brilliant makeup artist named Alexis. She would tease me because I always did my own hair and makeup. "Don't you trust me?" she would say. Truthfully, I was too scared to ask someone to do my hair and makeup, and I didn't think I was important enough to have someone to do it for me. I look back on it and curse myself. Alexis must've thought I enjoyed looking like the younger version of Bea Arthur on *The Golden Girls*.

Alexis and I would talk during commercial breaks on the weekend when she would touch up the main anchors. She knew I wasn't happy at the Imus job and this weekend gig wasn't ideal, so she asked if she could help. She mentioned she also worked at a cable news channel called Fox News. She had a lot of friends who worked there. Did she want me to pass along a tape or résumé? Alexis was close with a fellow makeup artist who knew the chairman and CEO of Fox News personally and might be able to help. I had no idea who Roger Ailes was, but if Alexis was happy over there, maybe I could be too. I brought my VHS, résumé, and lucky modeling headshot in with me the following weekend and handed it over.

Her friend and colleague was named Fouzia. Fouzia knew Mr. Ailes because he had personally helped her become a makeup artist. She started out at Fox cleaning offices, including his. Mr. Ailes asked her one day if there was something else she wanted to do. She told him she wanted to learn how to do makeup, and he offered to help. True to his word, he helped Fouzia go to beauty school, and she's still working at Fox today. Sometimes I get emotional when I see her because I remember how she helped me get the best job of my life. She told me one day while she was doing my makeup that she had a good feeling about me despite having never met me.

"Everyone needs some help finding their way sometimes," she said.

I tell people getting into the television business—or any career, for that matter—to always be kind to everyone they meet. You never know where your next job is going to come from. The hair and makeup artists are some of the most talented, smart, creative people I know. They have such a gift. Not only do they transform us visually, but they also become some of our closest confidantes. They are the first people we see in the morning; they've seen us at our best and our worst. They are our therapists and our pastors. I've prayed with some of them when I've had a bad day. I've broken down in tears with them. They know about fights I've had with my family or friends. I've laughed my head off and bawled my eyes out with them. I had one of my makeup artists tell me she knew I was pregnant even before I took the pregnancy test (not kidding), and they have cried with me when I was having a miscarriage. I used to promise if I wrote a book there would be a chapter called "Always Be Nice to the Hair and Makeup People."

A couple of days after I handed over my tape and résumé package to Alexis, I got a call asking me to come in and meet the CEO of the Fox News Channel, Roger Ailes. It was the fall of 2003. I remember what I wore that day: a light-green silk pantsuit. Yep. Me and Hillary Clinton, keeping the pantsuit industry alive and well.

I saw a *New Yorker* magazine that had a story about Mr. Ailes in it from a few weeks before. Ken Auletta did a thorough essay on him and the Fox News empire. It was required reading, and I'm glad I read it, because as soon as I walked into Roger's office, he asked me if I had seen it.

I told him I had, and it was impressive. I loved the fact that he began his career in radio like I did. He asked me what I took in school. I said I had gone to Carleton University in Ottawa, majoring in journalism, but I quit weeks later because I found out it wasn't until the fourth year that I would get to be a reporter and get out into the field. I was impatient. He laughed and told me it was probably the smartest thing I had ever done. I then told him a year later I had gone back to school and taken radio-television broadcasting at a local college and gotten a job in radio right away. Mr. Ailes loved stories of underdogs or scrappy people who didn't get their careers the conventional way. He went from digging ditches in Ohio to being the most powerful man in cable news.

Roger knew me from *Imus in the Morning*. He watched sometimes.

I remember he asked if I was a model. I saw he had my modeling headshot on his desk—the same one taken when I was in my twenties and twenty pounds lighter that I included with every résumé. I told him I was a model for about a year, and then I got hungry and needed to eat a hamburger.

He told me I was very funny—and good TV. He liked that I had a "naughty" side. Was I like that in real life? I truthfully told him I was playing a character and was ready for a new role. Imus was not the nicest person to work with.

My takeaway from the first meeting with Roger was that he was funny and charming and had a twinkle in his eye. I remember looking around his office and thinking how clean and orderly it was. There were several televisions on with the sound off. He said he could tell people were going to be stars just by looking at them on the screen without the volume.

I don't remember much more about that first meeting. He said he liked what he saw on TV, and that I had a "wicked sense of humor." He mentioned that he didn't know where he would put me at Fox, but he would think about it and get back to me.

A few days later I got a call from Mr. Ailes's secretary asking if I could meet with him at the Renaissance Times Square Hotel in the bar-restaurant area around 3:00 p.m. I thought it was a strange meeting place, but maybe he wanted to go "off campus."

I went to our designated area and waited for him to arrive. I saw him walk in and got up to greet him. He asked if I wanted to sit and get a drink. I thought this was odd, but it was after 3:00 p.m. and I didn't want to be rude. I ordered chardonnay, and he had the same.

We made small talk. He asked how I was and said I looked nice and that he wanted to get to know me a little better. After our wine was brought to the table, he reached over and grabbed my hand. And held it. Like a date. Did I have a boyfriend? (I did: I was seeing Sean.)

Was it serious? He was still holding my hand awkwardly across the table and asked if I had thought about him after our last meeting. I gently took my hand out of his and took a big gulp of wine. I told him I was excited at the idea of coming to work with him at Fox while thinking to myself: *This is a very strange job interview.*

He then asked: If he hired me, how would I see him in my life? I was taken aback, obviously, and told him perhaps as a *boss*? He laughed and said, "Well, I guess that too." I said I would look to him as a mentor, someone who could help me achieve my career goals. I don't know what else we talked about. The meeting didn't last much longer. He asked for the check and said he had to get back to the office. He joked that it probably wouldn't be good if someone saw us together like this.

He did say he was still very interested in me. He had to think about it a little more.

Mr. Ailes left, and I was bewildered. He never propositioned me, but was he hitting on me? Maybe he was just lonely. Perhaps he was testing me somehow, seeing what I would do when he asked me inappropriate questions?

I recently asked my former agent if I had told her about my meetings with Roger before I was hired. She said no, I hadn't, but she had always wondered if anything had happened after all the harassment stuff came out. She told me she always thought I was his "type" and she wasn't surprised he had hired me.

I did tell my therapist about my meeting with Roger, and eventually I also told Sean. I told several of my friends, including Megyn Kelly. We shared our Roger Ailes stories years before the Gretchen Carlson lawsuit.

I got a call from Ailes's secretary again a few days later. I was in my apartment when the phone rang.

"Hi, Miss Dean? I'm calling for Mr. Ailes. Do you have a moment to talk with him?"

I said sure. He got on the phone. "Janice Dean! How ya doing? How's that asshole Imus?"

I told him I was ready to move back to Canada any day now.

He asked what I was doing right then. "Talking to you?" I answered. And then he laughed.

"You're right! You are. Lucky you."

Pause.

"So, how are you at phone sex?"

WHAT!? Did I hear him right? Did he ask me how I was at phone sex?

My comedic instinct kicked in and I treated it like a joke.

"I'M TERRIBLE!"

"Really? You don't seem like you'd be terrible. You're a little naughty. I see that side of you. You've played phone sex with your boyfriends before, right? Let me hear what you'd say to him . . . like if I was your boyfriend."

I tried to laugh it off and said, "Mr. Ailes, this isn't a 1–900 number."

There was a pause. And then he laughed. Thank God. He laughed.

"Okay—well, maybe next time." Back to boss mode: "So, look, I've been thinking about this. Where I'd put you on Fox. Have you ever done the weather before?"

I was still trying to get the phone sex comment out of my mind, but he thankfully changed the subject.

"Well, yes," I said. "I did weather right out of college at the local television station in my hometown."

"Well, good. I've been looking for a daytime weather person. I think you'd be great. Call your agent. Kevin Magee, my VP of news programming, will be in touch, and we'll get you over here."

"Okay, wow. Great. Thank you!"

And that's how I got hired at Fox News.

I'm sure some of you are asking why I took the job if this guy was making weird suggestive remarks. The truth is, I never really thought he was serious. He was married and had a family. My situation was: I needed to get out of my current job immediately. I never thought I was in danger or he would ever try anything. Also, I wasn't attracted to him at all.

However, I was beginning to think every job came with weirdos saying and doing inappropriate things.

During the last few months before joining Fox, I had a colleague at WFAN who was also creeping me out. He would come into the newsroom and start massaging my shoulders in front of everyone. I found this weird, but I let him do it. He made it sound like he was helping me because I was so stressed-out from the job. Looking back, I didn't think he was doing it because he was attracted to me. The guy had a wife and kids. I never ever got a vibe that he was trying to hit on me.

Before I gave my notice, I was in the coworker's office talking to him about something. I remember what I was wearing that day. It was a dark-green leather jacket that was unbuttoned with jeans and a tank top. I wasn't wearing a bra because the tank top had one built into the fabric. I had lost weight and felt good enough to wear something that showed off my figure. We were wrapping up our discussion, and he walked over to the chair I was sitting in like he was going to give me a massage. He began rubbing my shoulders and telling me how tense I was. I started to get up to leave, and he grabbed my breasts underneath my leather jacket. He made a disgusting noise. It lasted only a few seconds, but that's all it took to imprint it on my brain forever. I was shocked. I froze. I didn't know what to do. I felt like I was going to throw up. Even now, writing this, the sick feeling returns. I was embarrassed and ashamed all at once. I got up and left his office. I may have told my friend Lou about this inappropriate behavior, since he and I were close friends. I told my therapist, Judy, and

I told Sean months later after I left the job. He told me it was a good thing I hadn't told him sooner. He would've probably killed the guy.

To this day I wonder, if I hadn't worn that outfit, would he have grabbed me like that? I realize now this is what victims do: blame themselves or something that they did for their harassers' behavior. I threw that outfit out immediately even though I had spent a few hundred dollars on the leather jacket.

I'm not sure if the colleague ever apologized. I tried to forget what he did, but as you can see, my memory of this is laser sharp.

The day I told the program director, Mark Chernoff, I was leaving for Fox News, and he asked if I could at least work through Christmas, doing the news for Charles as they played "The Best of Imus." Mark went into Imus's studio to tell him I was leaving during the show. I was writing his business report and was about to walk it into the studio when I heard Imus through the speakers on the air:

"So, Chernoff just came in to tell me that pig Janice Dean is leaving us to go to Fox. What a jerk. She never had the decency to tell me—just went behind my back. Hey, Chernoff, tell her she is not welcome in here ever again. I never want to see that fat face of hers again. What a backstabbing weasel. She sucked anyway. Fox can have her."

Part of me was relieved. I didn't want to see his disgusting face, either, ever again.

Kevin Magee wrote me an email as soon as he heard what Imus was saying on the air. He was listening because he knew I was going to give my notice that day and, knowing Imus, was on alert for what was unfolding live on radio and MSNBC.

"JD, are you okay? Can I call a car and get you the hell out of there? So glad you're coming over to work with us. The torture is almost over."

I said I was okay. "Thank you for reaching out."

For the last few days of my Imus nightmare, I stayed out of his way, and when I did news or traffic reports, he never commented. I was banished to a different studio.

Over the years I've had so many people come up and tell me they used to listen to me on *Imus*. Many of them tell me they enjoyed the show when I was on and missed me when I left. They thought it was a better show with me as a cast member. I look at that period of my career as very dark. But soon after that, the sun came out.

Sometimes you have to fight through some bad days to earn the best days of your life.

When I look back on the time with Imus, I try to remember that if it hadn't been for that job, I would've never met my husband, had my kids, and become the happy person I am today.

A few years after I started at Fox, Imus was fired for his comments about the Rutgers women's basketball team, calling them "nappy-headed hos." I went to media relations to ask if I could do an interview with a magazine about how horrible Imus was to me. I felt like I had so many things I could say to make sure a guy like him would never be mean to another woman. They thought it was a great idea. Maybe we could do something for *Vanity Fair*. We met in Mr. Ailes's office and pitched him the concept. Roger knew how badly Imus had treated me. It was the reason why I was looking for a new job when he hired me at Fox. He immediately said no, and reasoned that the article would put the attention on me instead of Imus, and he didn't think that was a good idea. Imus had been fired; his career was over. Mine was just beginning. Why would I ruin that by doing a smear piece?

I was in tears and said, "But what if I was your daughter? Don't you think I should tell my story about how horrible he was to me to warn others?" Roger still said no. Best to leave it. Then he actually said:

"Save it for your book someday."

Roger hired Imus in 2009 to host the morning show on the Fox

Business channel. I was horrified and felt betrayed. Mr. Ailes knew how badly Imus treated me. I went to my boss at the time and told him under no circumstances would I ever appear on Imus's show to do the weather. There were a couple of times over the years, especially during hurricane season, when Fox Business would request me to do weather on his show. As much as I am the biggest team player, I refused. There is no way in hell I would ever be on the air with that man ever again. I did see him in the hallway once. He looked miserable, old, and unhealthy. I, on the other hand, was happy, confident, and smiling—on the outside and on the inside.

Chapter 8

IT'S COMPLICATED

I didn't see Roger Ailes right away. I went in and met with Kevin Magee, who oversaw programming. He was terrific. He mentioned that Roger liked me a lot, and it was a direct order to get me over to Fox. Had I done weather before?

I told him I had done some part-time weather presenting out of college at the local CBC station and I did weather reports on the radio when I did the news. He thought maybe I should do a little training with a company up in Boston that had meteorologists that Fox used on the weekend. They didn't have their own in-house daytime weather person. I would be their first official "Foxcaster."

I did some rehearsals, refreshing my green screen skills, and then we had a big January nor'easter heading up the East Coast. This would be my first official day on the air.

After my first weather report, I was called up to Roger's office. He got up and hugged me, and put his cheek out to give him a kiss.

"Great job out there. Congratulations. Happy to have you here. Let me look at you!" He asked me how it felt, and I told him I was nervous but I thought it had gone okay.

Then he asked me to sit with him at the back of his office where he had a couch. He said he was glad I was there. I was something special, and he would help me. I just needed to loosen up a bit: "Show more of your personality. Come out of your shell . . ."

When I look back at the meetings I would have with Roger in his office, I never felt he was going to do anything physical with me. There was one time where I went to give him a kiss on the cheek and he moved his face so that my mouth ended up close to his. I was a little taken aback, but I wasn't alarmed. He would make suggestive remarks, and, yes, I was told to "spin" for him. He made it sound like "just turn around, let me look at you."

We all had meetings with Roger. The hair and makeup people knew right away that we had to "go see the boss" if we came in halfway through our shift and asked to be touched up before going up to the second floor.

When all the harassment stuff had come out, and Gretchen launched her lawsuit in 2016, I recall talking to a former anchor about doing the "spin," something many of us were asked to do when we would go up to Roger's office. The anchor told me she wasn't bothered by the spin. After all, we were in a visual business, and our bodies were on display. Why should we be ashamed of it? She had had a couple of kids, and she worked hard to look good. She was proud of her body, and took it as a compliment. Other women thought it was shameful and demeaning. I understand both sides.

He was definitely inappropriate. He liked to curse, and he had a crude sense of humor.

I remember him making comments on several occasions about how I should never get married. The sex was boring afterward.

I would always try to change the subject or make a joke. Thank God, I could always make a joke.

The one thing we all knew was not to cross him or get him angry. You did not want Roger Ailes as an enemy. He was the king. Fox was his kingdom. Nothing was on the air that wasn't okayed by him. Everyone reported to Roger. If he saw you on television and didn't like what you were wearing or the color of your lipstick, there was a call, and you were told immediately to fix it. When I wrote my series of children's books, he had to give the okay. I was told that in the acknowledgments at the back of every book he had to be the first one I thanked. That was fine. I wouldn't be writing children's books if I didn't have my job at Fox. He was the reason I was there.

A few months into my new weather job, I asked him if I could try some anchoring. I had done news writing and announcing with Imus and back home in Canada. At that time in my career I wanted to do other things and prove myself.

Roger told me he would set it up with one of his trusted producers. I could do a screen test but I couldn't tell anyone. It would be our secret, because he knew other female anchors would get "very jealous" of our relationship. He said we would watch my audition tapes and work closely together.

I did a few shifts as a host and did overnight news cut-ins for a couple of years, but I never asked Roger to look at the tapes with me. I enjoyed doing it but decided eventually I wanted to focus on my weather job. Maybe in the back of my mind I felt it might've led to more uncomfortable situations.

Sometimes producers would tell me Roger would single me out in meetings and say how great I was doing. "Put her on TV more," he would say.

No one except Roger Ailes would ever think of hiring a woman from Ottawa, Canada, to be the daytime weather person on the number one cable news channel. I am grateful he hired me. By the same token, we know Roger had a dark side, as many powerful men do. I don't believe he was all evil. However, he did use his power to manipulate.

What Roger did when I was first being hired was inappropriate and wrong. I think he was testing me to see if I would take the bait. In other words, when he made suggestive remarks, would I return the sentiment? I never did, and I would tap-dance and think of other ways to get myself out of a compromising situation. He never went over the line like my colleague at WFAN did in his office, touching me physically.

He definitely did cross the line, and we now know he did some awful things to some of the women employees, many of whom will never tell their stories because of nondisclosure agreements.

But Mr. Ailes had another side to him. He could be kind and helpful. People who worked for him loved him. He was loyal to the people he hired. He would ask some, like Fouzia, if there were other jobs they wanted to try, and he would make it happen. He believed in the American Dream especially for those who he thought deserved it.

Roger would always tell me I never had to work anywhere else ever again. I would always have a job at Fox. He was supportive when I was diagnosed with MS and told me he would help in any way I needed. When I went up to his office to tell him I was pregnant with each of my children, he smiled and said what a wonderful thing it was, having kids. He knew I would make a good mom.

After my first year at Fox, my meetings with him in his office became less frequent. He left me alone. I just thought maybe he had liked me in a romantic way but thankfully it had worn off. I was relieved he had lost interest and I could focus on the job I was hired to do.

When I visit students at schools, I tell them to always be nice to people. It doesn't matter who they are or what they do. You never know where kindness will lead. For me, it was an incredible makeup artist named Alexis who befriended me and knew I needed to find another job. Always be nice to the hair and makeup people.

Sadly, there is a tragic end to this part of the story as well.

My friend Alexis, who helped bring me to Fox News, died tragically in 2014 on Christmas Eve in a car crash. She was driving from New Jersey to Florida to be with her family for the holidays. Her youngest daughter, Sophia, and nephew were in the car, and thankfully they survived. Alexis was ejected from the car upon impact. She was killed instantly. I got a call from one of the audio engineers when the news broke. I cried for a long time. Then I called Ray, her husband, to see if I could do anything. He was still in shock and processing the information. I told him I loved him and I loved Alexis and to call if he needed anything. Ray had met Alexis at Fox. We were all so happy they found each other, and they had their beautiful daughter, Sophia, who was still a toddler when Alexis died. Her older daughter, Xianna, is the spitting image of her mama and has the exact same warm smile and kind spirit.

I'm so glad Alexis spent the last few years of her life with a wonderful, kind man.

I still think of Alexis often, especially when I see Fouzia. They were so generous and good to me. They are the reason I am at Fox News, and they are the reason I can provide for my family every day. If it weren't for Alexis and Fouzia, I'm not sure where I'd be. I know I wouldn't be this happy and feel loved both at home and at work.

In my heart I know Alexis is in heaven, making her fellow angels smile and lending a hand. Maybe even introducing good people to each other, making a difference, and certainly making them all look their best.

Chapter 9

FOXCASTING

When I first started at Fox, I was hired as the daytime weather reporter. Kevin Magee, who oversaw Fox News programming, came up with the term "Foxcaster." I had done weather before during my CBC fill-in days, but I was a little rusty, and that was weather in Canada, a different country with provinces and territories and temperatures that were in Celsius. I had to get accustomed to all the states, cities, and geographic landmarks. Roger saw me and Shep Smith as being a team on his show *Studio B*, so I would rehearse with him before I officially went to air. Shep, by the way, is the one that came up with my nickname "Janice Dean the weather machine." It was during our rehearsals one day that he started calling me that, out of the blue. I didn't mind at all. It was fun and catchy, and the name stuck. My friend Jane Skinner would be on doing the news, and she had a feature called "Skinnerville" every day where they would talk about a fun water cooler story. My weather machine segment usually followed "Skinnerville" and many times there would be cookies or brownies for the staff and crew, because Jane loved to bake and bring in snacks.

I covered a lot of big weather stories over my fifteen years as a forecaster and meteorologist. There were several catastrophic tornado outbreaks that I recall instantly.

The 2011 Joplin tornado ravaged the city of Joplin, Missouri, and surrounding areas as an EF5 with winds of over 200 miles per hour. The tornado killed 158 people and injured more than 1,000 others. It ranks as the costliest single tornado in US history and was the deadliest tornado in sixty years, the seventh deadliest overall.

Then came Moore, Oklahoma, in May 2013. An EF5 destroyed part of that town with winds of 210 mph killing two dozen and injuring over 200. We were showing live video of the huge funnel cloud touching down near two elementary schools. I remember seeing the yellow school buses with a backdrop of a giant black wall of destruction devouring everything in its path. It was in this tornado that seven third-grade students died. That's when I get choked up—knowing children are terrified inside their schools without their parents. I've gotten upset many times on air while trying to cover disasters and realizing the toll it takes on people and their communities. It's always after the disaster, however, when you see neighbors helping neighbors, strangers lending a hand, and how it's times like these when people come together to rebuild homes and each other.

I also was part of hurricane coverage in the historic 2005 season, the year of Katrina. Katrina was the eleventh named storm and the fifth hurricane that year. It strengthened to a Category 5 hurricane with sustained winds of 175 miles per hour. I remember seeing the "certain death" bulletin from the National Weather Service in New Orleans that left little doubt this storm was going to put residents in mortal danger. I thought it was important to read this live during my weather report. My producer, Tom Lowell, gave me time to recite the entire thing word for word. It was after Katrina had rapidly strengthened into a Cat 5 monster. Robert Ricks was the meteorologist who wrote it:

URGENT—WEATHER MESSAGE

NATIONAL WEATHER SERVICE NEW ORLEANS LA

1011 AM CDT SUN AUG 28, 2005

. . . DEVASTATING DAMAGE EXPECTED . . .

HURRICANE KATRINA . . . A MOST POWERFUL HURRICANE WITH UNPRECEDENTED STRENGTH . . . RIVALING THE INTENSITY OF HURRICANE CAMILLE OF 1969.

MOST OF THE AREA WILL BE UNINHABITABLE FOR WEEKS . . . PERHAPS LONGER. AT LEAST ONE HALF OF WELL CONSTRUCTED HOMES WILL HAVE ROOF AND WALL FAILURE. ALL GABLED ROOFS WILL FAIL . . . LEAVING THOSE HOMES SEVERELY DAMAGED OR DESTROYED.

THE MAJORITY OF INDUSTRIAL BUILDINGS WILL BECOME NON FUNCTIONAL. PARTIAL TO COMPLETE WALL AND ROOF FAILURE IS EXPECTED. ALL WOOD FRAMED LOW RISING APARTMENT BUILDINGS WILL BE DESTROYED. CONCRETE BLOCK LOW RISE APARTMENTS WILL SUSTAIN MAJOR DAMAGE . . . INCLUDING SOME WALL AND ROOF FAILURE.

HIGH RISE OFFICE AND APARTMENT BUILDINGS WILL SWAY DANGEROUSLY . . . A FEW TO THE POINT OF TOTAL COLLAPSE. ALL WINDOWS WILL BLOW OUT.

AIRBORNE DEBRIS WILL BE WIDESPREAD . . . AND MAY INCLUDE HEAVY ITEMS SUCH AS HOUSEHOLD APPLIANCES AND EVEN LIGHT VEHICLES. SPORT UTILITY VEHICLES AND LIGHT TRUCKS WILL BE MOVED. THE BLOWN DEBRIS WILL CREATE ADDITIONAL DESTRUCTION. PERSONS . . . PETS . . . AND LIVESTOCK EXPOSED TO THE WINDS WILL FACE CERTAIN DEATH IF STRUCK.

POWER OUTAGES WILL LAST FOR WEEKS . . . AS MOST POWER POLES WILL BE DOWN AND TRANSFORMERS DESTROYED. WATER SHORTAGES WILL MAKE HUMAN SUFFERING INCREDIBLE BY MODERN STANDARDS.

THE VAST MAJORITY OF NATIVE TREES WILL BE SNAPPED OR UPROOTED. ONLY THE HEARTIEST WILL REMAIN STANDING . . . BUT BE TOTALLY DEFOLIATED. FEW CROPS WILL REMAIN. LIVESTOCK LEFT EXPOSED TO THE WINDS WILL BE KILLED.

AN INLAND HURRICANE WIND WARNING IS ISSUED WHEN SUSTAINED WINDS NEAR HURRICANE FORCE . . . OR FREQUENT GUSTS AT OR ABOVE HURRICANE FORCE . . . ARE CERTAIN WITHIN THE NEXT 12 TO 24 HOURS.

ONCE TROPICAL STORM AND HURRICANE FORCE WINDS ONSET . . . DO NOT VENTURE OUTSIDE!

Hurricane Katrina killed more than 1,800 people, left hundreds of thousands homeless, and destroyed parts of the Gulf Coast. Katrina produced the highest storm surge ever recorded on the US coast: an unbelievable 27.9 feet at Pass Christian, Mississippi. It was this storm that overwhelmed some of the levees and floodwalls that were there to protect the city of New Orleans. More than fifty of them failed as a record-setting storm surge from Katrina crashed into the coastline.

Shep Smith reported from NOLA with incredible images and heartbreaking stories. It was the worst weather disaster in the US, and I covered it in just my second year of being hired at Fox News Channel. When I'm asked what is the worst weather event I've ever covered, there is no comparison. Hurricane Katrina was a tragedy of epic proportions, and not just in a weather context: the way it was handled by government officials was also a giant catastrophe.

The year 2017 was a historic one for tropical weather as well. Hurricane Harvey brought a record 60.58 inches of rain in southeast Texas. I was texting my friends from Houston Karen, George, and Allison beforehand making sure they were prepared for a possible disaster. I even told them to make sure they had an axe to cut themselves out of the roof of their homes if they had to. The impact was devastating, and Harvey is now tied with Hurricane Katrina as the costliest tropical cyclone on record with $125 billion in damages. My friends Karen and George were out of their home for a year while it had to be rebuilt.

In October 2018, Hurricane Michael completely devastated the panhandle and big bend coast of Florida. This storm was the most intense hurricane to strike the US coast since Andrew in 1992, and the third most intense hurricane in terms of pressure after the 1935 Labor Day Hurricane and Camille in 1969. Not only that, but it was the fourth strongest (155 mph winds) landfalling hurricane in the US and the strongest to hit the Florida Panhandle. The area around the eyewall where Michael made landfall completely obliterated communities. The aerial footage afterward was similar to a war zone. Many gulf residents that lived through Katrina say the damage was reminiscent of what they went through back in 2005. When the pictures and video come in after a storm has struck, that's when it hits home that sometimes you have absolutely no control over what is about to happen in your life. No matter how well you prepare yourself.

One of the other biggest forecast moments for me personally and professionally was Hurricane Sandy. On October 25, 2012, my producer Brandon Noriega and I were looking at the latest forecast models from the National Hurricane Center right before the 11:00 a.m. advisory. The European computer model predicted the storm would turn west and strike the New York–New Jersey region rather than turn east and head out to sea, which is the usual trajectory this late in the season. Cold fronts typically come off the East Coast and sweep the storm out into the Atlantic away from land—especially in the fall months this far north. The other computer models had this out-to-sea scenario. The Euro model was remarkably accurate with this northeast landfall outcome over a week in advance, but we never rely on just one computer model. We watch several different forecast outcomes and take a consensus, which is why you see a wide spread in that "cone of uncertainty" showing a hurricane track five days out.

By the 11:00 a.m. advisory on the twenty-fifth, the National Hurricane Center track officially showed the system moving into the Northeast. As a Cat 2 or strong Cat 1 storm, damage could potentially be devastating for this region.

The storm at that point was still in the Bahamas, but now the tracks were showing a sharp left-hand hook several days out right into the Northeast with a bull's-eye of New York City. I had a weather report coming up at around 11:30 on the show *Happening Now* with an update on the forecast, but I knew this latest path was going to make news particularly for the millions of people around New York City. I called the senior producer, Clint Henderson, and told him we needed to be the lead story. Clint knew me well enough that if I was telling him weather should be the lede, I wasn't fooling around. Brandon updated the graphics showing the hurricane moving into the Northeast, and I went to air. *Washington Post* reporter Erik Wemple later transcribed my warning word for word for his blog, in which he singled me out for "breaking from the pack" of all other meteorologists and being way more dramatic than everyone else.

I was one of the first on-air broadcast meteorologists to warn people of Sandy and the possible outcome of the storm hitting the Northeast. My stern message and forecast on the hurricane was not scripted. People are shocked to learn meteorologists don't use a teleprompter. We are ad-libbing everything, so if we screw anything up, there are no writers or producers to fall back on. Yes, my warning was dire. However, I wouldn't say I was frothing at the mouth. I've always said I would rather people be overly cautious and prepare for the worst. I'll take the heat if the forecast is wrong. I'd rather have people prepared than caught off guard.

Mr. Wemple then added this nugget at the end of his column:

> Fox News's Dean could well be right in ringing the bell more loudly than other media outlets. Perhaps Dean and Fox News have better information about the storm and are throwing caution to the (very strong) wind, the better to protect a densely populated region. Another possibility is that the hyperventilation of Fox News's political coverage blows into its weather coverage as well. Events should clarify this matter.

Hurricane Sandy hit the Northeast coast on October 29. It was the largest Atlantic hurricane on record, measuring over 1,000 miles in diameter. If you look at the satellite presentation on a map before it made landfall, it is breathtaking to see how huge this storm was.

Sandy was the most destructive of the 2012 season with nearly

$70 billion in damage (2012 USD). It's the fourth costliest hurricane on record behind Katrina (2005), Harvey (2017), and Maria (2017).

There were 233 fatalities as a result of Sandy. Coastal flooding from the storm resulted in a public transit shutdown that stranded 11 million commuters without service.

Looking back on my "dire" forecast, and watching the video of that 11:00 a.m. weather report, I would not change a thing. If I need to get our viewers' attention about a storm that could be dangerous then I'm going to put all my energy into warning people and telling them the possible worst-case scenario.

While I was reporting on Hurricane Sandy, I was staying in the city for many nights while Sean had to take care of the kids at home. It was tough to be working while I was worried that my own family could be affected by the storm. Our power went out for several days, and there was damage to our neighborhood, but, thankfully, we are prepared as a family for weather emergencies. I like to practice what I preach! The toughest part was not being with them. First responders and people whose jobs require them to be out helping others can relate to this. I'll never forget what it felt like to finally come home on Halloween to see my kids in their costumes trick-or-treating around the neighborhood. I couldn't wait to see them, and I hugged them both so hard with tears bursting from my eyes. Many people were shell-shocked after being home for days with no power. Trees were still down with some streets blocked off. But it's always during these days and weeks after a storm that I see the best of humanity. I was grateful to Sean and my friends for being there while Mom was at work trying to forecast and warn those in the storm's path.

Over the years, people have asked me if I want to go out and report in a hurricane. My answer is always "no." There's nothing wrong with meteorologists that do, but for me, it feels odd being someone who tells people to heed warnings and stay away from a storm while at the same time not listening to my own advice. And there have been times both on air and off air where I will get mad at reporters that are clearly in danger and tell them to seek higher ground or get out of their live location. I can't help it. It really upsets me seeing one of my friends or coworkers possibly moments away from being hit by flying debris or being overtopped by a storm surge. I understand the predicament—we need to show how terrible these forces of nature can be, but no live shot is worth risking your life.

Now, if it's a blizzard or snowstorm here in New York, that's a different story. I've covered many of those over the years and I enjoy it a great deal. As long as you're not on the road trying to travel, and you're prepared for power outages with a safe place to stay warm, you shouldn't get into too much trouble in a blizzard. Every year I get my husband to take video of me performing the first snow angel of the season. And you'll also see me do this whenever there's a snowstorm on *Fox & Friends*. I will continue to perfect my snow angels every single year even if I live to be a hundred.

After what would become the worst hurricane season on record in the US back in 2005, I decided that if weathercaster was going to be my full-time career, I should investigate going back to school to become a broadcast meteorologist. My good friend and colleague Rick Reichmuth had told me about meteorology courses he had taken with the Mississippi State University distance learning program, whereby many broadcast meteorologists got credits to apply for the American Meteorological Society (AMS) "seal of approval."

It took me three years to complete all the courses required to get the seal, which is described as recognizing on-air meteorologists for "sound delivery of weather information to the general public." I did online exams during my summer vacations and even on my honeymoon to Paris at one point. I then had to do an on-air component of forecasting for several days that was sent to a board of meteorologists, who determined if I was good enough in my presentation to be granted the AMS seal.

My experience shows that it's never too late to go back to school to learn something new. I think it works in my favor that I had a broadcasting career before that honed my ad-libbing skills. You can be the smartest meteorologist in the room, crunching numbers and doing equations, but if you can't communicate a message on television or radio properly, then it's going to be tough to succeed in this business.

Even though I didn't set out with the specific goal of being an on-camera weatherperson, I am so grateful for the opportunity I've been given. I certainly have opinions on the news of the day, politics, and what's going on in the world, but I always say my job is to tell you the forecast: fair and balanced. East Coast, West Coast, and everywhere in between. The only red and blue I see on my maps is when I'm talking about areas of low or high pressure. And if there's time for a little dancing, an impromptu snow angel, the latest on pet fashion, or National Pancake Day, you can bet I'm going to cover that too.

Chapter 10

LEARNING I HAVE MS, THE "MY, YOU LOOK SO WELL" DISEASE

My life wasn't perfect, but it was getting better all the time. I loved my work. I was busier than ever. Not only was 2005 the year of Katrina, but we had Hurricanes Dennis, Emily, Rita, and Wilma. We had so many storms, for the first time in its history, the National Hurricane Center had to go to the Greek alphabet to name them. I was working long hours and found myself feeling overwhelmingly tired. I chalked it up to lack of sleep for weeks on end and depression from all the devastation we were seeing on television. Little did I know that as I was warning people of the next hurricane, my body was dealing with its own neurological storm, one that had been forming for years.

I took time off and decided to go back home to Canada with Sean for a week. The first day of my vacation I woke up to numbness in my feet and parts of my legs. I felt like I couldn't get out of bed from exhaustion. I had no idea what was wrong.

I went to a doctor in my hometown to see if she could figure it out. She was blunt and honest. "This could be anything from a slipped disc to multiple sclerosis. You should get back to the US to see a neurologist."

I thought she was crazy. *MS? Isn't that the wheelchair disease?* I took her advice, though. When I got back to New York, I made an appointment to meet with a rather unemotional and very detached neurologist.

He took one look at my MRIs and decided to give me a most unpleasant spinal tap in his office right away. I was by myself in one of those hospital gowns open from the back as this robo-doctor was putting a gigantic needle into my spine. Tears rolled down my face.

Dr. Distant came in and asked if I wanted to call a family member to come and pick me up, and he would go over the results with me. I called Sean, and asked if he would come. I remember my teeth were chattering, but I couldn't tell if it was because I was cold from wearing an open hospital gown or scared to death.

We sat holding hands as he told us the news.

"It would appear you have multiple sclerosis."

In every single technical term possible, Dr. Feelbad told us the MRIs had shown lesions (abnormal damage on an organ or tissue) on both my brain and spine. He pointed these out on my scan. Then he showed us the paperwork that showed I had the protein or oligoclonal banding they look for in MS patients. He had extracted this finding from that god-awful spinal tap. The presence of these bands suggested inflammation of the central nervous system.

In simpler terms, my explanation of MS is this:

Multiple sclerosis is a disease in which the immune system eats away at the protective covering of the nerves. We don't know why. The fatty substance that protects our nerves is called myelin. This is similar to the plastic coating that covers electrical wires to keep everything together. Wires that lose their insulation can "short out"—so when our immune system eats away at that protective coating, messages can get fuzzy as they are transmitted from our nerves to our brain. When I wake up at night from a random shooting pain, I chalk it up to my body having an electrical storm.

Sean asked questions, and I tried to listen, but truthfully I completely zoned out. How did these little injuries get there? Why did my body hate itself enough to hurt itself? Had I done something wrong? I started imagining myself in a wheelchair.

The doctor gave me steroids to help with the numbness and tingling and told me I more than likely had multiple sclerosis, but we'd have to wait and see over the next few months, since I had to have another "episode" to diagnose it officially. We'd have to book another appointment for more MRIs in the next six months.

I couldn't believe this man who had half a dozen diplomas on his wall couldn't tell me for sure what I had or if it would come back or how bad it could be. Turns out, predicting what MS does isn't any easier than forecasting the weather six months in advance.

I also wished he had taken an acting class to at least look compassionate.

I went home from my worst doctor visit of all time and was depressed for days. My boyfriend, Sean, was incredible, but I was also preparing myself for the possibility that he would leave me at any moment. Who would want to hang around and deal with this Debbie Downer with a dire diagnosis? I knew I had to tell the people at work and was very nervous about it, because I had been on the job for only a year and I was still trying to prove myself. A close friend who was in the business told me not to tell anyone at Fox because that would probably be the end of my career. But I have always felt I need to be honest. How could I hide this? I called my boss, the man who had hired me a little over a year ago, and told him.

"Roger Ailes, please."

His secretary asked who was calling.

"It's Janice Dean," I said, trying not to cry.

She told me he was in a meeting and would call me back. And he did.

"Janice . . . what's going on?" he said in his gruff Roger voice.

I tried to keep my voice steady and told him about the possible diagnosis. I had knots in my stomach. I think as soon as I said "MS," the tears came.

He was very kind and understanding. Roger could be like that— sound very fatherly. He told me not to worry, to take my time, and to call if I needed anything. He also suggested I talk to Neil Cavuto. He was the funny, smart business anchor who hosted *Your World* on Fox. I didn't know Neil well, but he loved to tease me when I did the weather with him on the air:

"Janice Dean, how do you guys still have a job when you're only 50 percent right?"

"I could ask the same about your stock picks, Neil!"

"Nicely done, JD."

Not only was Neil an anchor, but he had a fancy title after his name.

He was the senior vice president, anchor, and managing editor. He hosted three television programs on the Fox News Channel and our sister network, Fox Business. He was also a cancer survivor and, I now remembered, living with multiple sclerosis.

Neil would be my first phone call after I went back to work.

I was off for several weeks before I could go back. Unfortunately, I was one of the 32 percent of people who get something called a "spinal headache" after that dreadful spinal tap. My spinal fluid was leaking through the puncture site. It was one of the most painful things I've ever had in my life. I could not sleep, eat, or sit still. I had to go back and get something called a blood patch, which I will spare you the details of. As gnarly as it sounds, it worked, and that horrible piercing, bloodcurdling headache went away.

Thankfully, the steroids started working as well, and the feeling started to come back in my feet and my thighs. I remember booking myself for a pedicure at the nail salon near my apartment and quietly sobbing because I could finally feel the lady scrubbing my feet, something I hadn't been able to feel a few weeks earlier. She asked why I was crying:

"Am I scrubbing too hard, miss?"

"No. Scrub as hard as you like," I responded. "It feels fantastic."

Now that I was feeling better, I decided to find another neurologist. I couldn't bear going back to Dr. Detached. This took me a few tries, and I like to joke to other MS patients that finding your doctor is kind of like dating: you have to go on a few of them until you find your match. I've been told this is a common complaint with MS patients. Having a chronic illness, you crave compassion. I don't necessarily need someone to hug me on every visit, but at least try to make eye contact.

In between my quest for the "one" (neurologist), I started reading every book I could get my hands on with a protagonist living with MS. The first was Richard M. Cohen's book *Blindsided: Lifting a Life Above Illness; A Reluctant Memoir*. Richard spent his career as a journalist and a television producer. It was beautifully written, but it scared the shit out of me. He warned against telling your employer you have MS. This was not what I wanted to hear. His struggles with the progressive side of MS were depressing and sometimes very angry. I ended up loving his wife, Meredith Vieira, even more after reading how wonderful a partner and caretaker she was.

I later got the chance to meet and talk to Richard when I interviewed him for an essay I was writing for Foxnews.com. We did a question-and-answer session at an MS function after I was newly diagnosed. Despite his challenges, he is funny and charming. We joked that doing these MS events all the time could lead to an MS flare-up, because as much as you want to help the cause, they can overbook you if you make yourself "too" available.

I also read Montel Williams's book about his life living with MS and the funny, beautiful Teri Garr had a more uplifting read about her MS. I banned myself from googling anything.

I wanted to read about people who were doing well despite the illness. Why weren't there any of these? The words "incurable," "chronic," "blind," and "wheelchair" were all I was seeing.

Perhaps I was looking for stories of miraculous recoveries, which unfortunately don't typically happen with MS.

When I finally went back to work, I could tell people had already heard about my diagnosis. I could read their faces when they saw me walking through the hallways. That sheepish "Hello" or "How are YOU doing?" I didn't blame them; I would've probably been the same way.

I then called Neil Cavuto, who told me to come to his office right away.

He dropped everything, turned off the TV, brought a chair over, and sat next to me. He kept a stream of tissues in motion, consoling me while I just cried and told him all my fears. What would happen to my career? My personal life? My self-esteem?

Neil calmed me down, promised me I was going to be okay, and reminded me that I was working at a great company that would support us, even if that support included building his-and-hers wheelchair ramps for us. He told a few jokes, too, which made me smile despite the black tears streaming down my face from too much mascara.

I'll never forget that day and what Neil did for me. And still does for me. He'll drop me a line once in a while asking, "How are you doing, kiddo? Doing great out there. Can you tell me the forecast for New Jersey this weekend?" We also joke with each other that we will use our illness to get out of every chore possible at home. "No putting out the garbage for us, my friend. We have MS!"

Nowadays, I try to follow Neil's lead and do the same for others. There have been several people over the years who have come up to me at Fox to tell me they've joined the MS club, and they weren't afraid to tell their bosses because I was there—setting an example, being on TV, doing weather, laughing, dancing, and singing despite the war that was going on inside my body.

I remember a fellow MS'er saying she calls it the "My, you look so well" disease, because you can look normal on the outside and no one knows that you might be in pain or have a weird burning sensation somewhere or have vision issues.

I tried to find more people to talk to who were living with MS. It was the one thing that kept me going: seeing others who were not just functioning but thriving.

Back to my quest to find my neurologist match: after my first dreadful doctor date, I went on another, this time with an NFL sports neurologist that my dear friend Jane Skinner had set up for me. (Jane and I worked together at Fox for six years, and she also happens to be married to the commissioner of the NFL, Roger Goodell. Needless to say, they have some pretty good connections when it comes to physicians.)

Jane offered to pick me up at my apartment on the Upper West Side and drive me all the way out to Lake Success, Long Island, to visit this big-time sports neurologist. Unfortunately, Jane and I got lost (these were the days just before GPS), and we were an hour late. I was stressed-out to begin with—on top of my already stressful possible diagnosis—and we could tell that this guy was not pleased that we weren't on time. I went into the office and burst into tears as soon as he mentioned how busy he was, and he was doing someone a favor by seeing me. Once he saw my tears, he softened up a little bit, but not much. The one thing this doctor recommended despite his terrible bedside manner was that I should be on medication right away. He wrote out a prescription and shuffled me out with some instructions. I saw my beautiful friend Jane in the waiting room, and a new round of fresh tears came.

There is a moral to this story—other than it helps to cry. When I do MS events in front of a crowd of doctors, I tell these stories about how it's not only important for MDs to know their stuff, it's almost as important to be compassionate with their patients. We know your time is precious and you have many other people to see, and sometimes life gets in the way. Still, you have people who are emotionally broken in your office. Try to spend a minute or two looking them in the eye and let them know you're there for them.

My third date was successful. I found a kind neurologist named Mark Tullman. His partner, Nurse Practitioner Jen Smrtka, and I have since become good friends, and she's the one that let me in on the fact that Dr. Tullman is sometimes referred to as Dr. McDreamy. I mean, it doesn't hurt that he's handsome. Truthfully, I didn't care about what he looked like, since he was good to me. He took the time to explain things, and was sympathetic to my fears while taking my vitals. I fell in love with Jen, who I call my angel in a white coat. She would calm my anxiety and point out how far we've come with this disease, telling me tales of strength and people overcoming challenges while holding my hand. Not only that, but we were around the same age and were able to gossip about dating, living in New York, and good skin care. God bless our nurses. I've met some great doctors in my life, but I've met some incredible, superhero nurses. That's what Jen was. We're still close even though she works with a different doctor and has moved to different cities over the years. She has been a source of goodness, light, and strength in a time of extreme darkness. And she still keeps up on the latest in skin care.

In 2007, I now had a great doctor and was getting the hang of the drugs I was on. Amazingly, I was still working full-time. I had to manage my sleep; keep cool, especially in the summertime; and I continued to have minor electrical malfunctions, but otherwise things were back to normal.

Maybe now was the time to tell my story. Perhaps I could share my diagnosis to help others. Maybe I could be the positive influence whom someone living with this unpredictable illness would look to— the person I had needed to see when I was first diagnosed.

I asked for a meeting with the VP of programming, to run my idea by him. Could I shoot a package of my doctors' visits and MRI appointments and report on how I'm living pretty well despite having MS? It might help others. Not missing a beat, he told me:

"No." He didn't think this was the time to discuss a diagnosis on television, let alone make a production out of it.

I was crushed and too shocked to press him on why he didn't think this was a good idea.

I decided that if programming didn't like my pitch, perhaps the news department would.

I emailed my concept to our VP of news. Right away, he thought it was a great idea and gave the green light. I then got a producer and camera crew together. They followed me to my MRI appointments, and we interviewed Dr. Tullman and my sweet friend Jen, for a report that would air on the news channel. Somewhere down the line the programming VP found out and wanted me to call him.

"Did you go behind my back and do this MS thing?"

I said I hadn't gone behind his back; I just wanted to ask someone else what he thought, and the news department thought it was a great idea.

I think he hung up the phone afterward.

In the end, I was grateful someone thought my "MS thing" was worthy.

From there, I pitched *Fox & Friends* weekend and *Fox Report* weekend. I came in and told my story and showed how I was living with MS but still doing relatively well. By going public with the illness, I was finally doing something I would've loved to have seen on television when I was first diagnosed.

Afterward, I got so many emails and words of encouragement from coworkers, friends, and viewers. Maybe the reason I was given this platform of television wasn't just to give weather forecasts but also to shed a little light on what's going on behind the scenes in someone's real life beyond the TV screen.

It was never my goal to be the poster girl for MS—although I don't mind boasting I was the official cover girl for *Neurology Now* magazine a few years back—but I do feel a calling to be someone who can help others identify and live with the disease.

I don't see Dr. McDreamy anymore. He lives in St. Louis with his family and is the director of clinical research at the MS Center for Innovations in Care.

Before he left me—and we had an amicable separation—Dr. Tullman kindly referred me to a friend and colleague he thought might be a good fit for me. Her name is Dr. Tracy DeAngelis, and I adore her. She always greets me with a smile and a hug when I see her, and when she asks me how I'm doing, she does it by looking me straight in the eye. She takes time with me, never looking at her watch, and takes copious notes old-school-style with a pen and yellow notepad. I'm grateful for her care.

So far on this journey, I've done all right. There have been trying moments, painful situations, and moments of feeling sorry for myself. However, being diagnosed with MS has also made me realize the important things in life. The days of climbing the career ladder for self-fulfillment, gratification, and self-esteem are over. My health, my family, and their happiness are far more important.

People ask if I'm as "sunny" in real life as I seem to be on television. I think part of the reason I'm so happy is that I learned pretty early on that your life can change in an instant.

I also believe the challenges you are presented with in life are there to help you discover who you are. It's the obstacles and adversity that make us stronger.

That and one of my favorite sayings: "What doesn't kill you . . . makes you blonder!" Ha!

Chapter 11

ZIN OWL

Life in New York was starting to look better despite the MS diagnosis that came shortly after being hired at Fox. Sean and I were doing well, my illness was in check, and I was enjoying my career again. Doing what I most loved to do, as my dad used to say.

I hadn't heard from him since our exchange when I was working with Imus, but one day I was writing on my weather blog, and I saw a name pop up in the comments section that I recognized: "Zin Owl." That was my dad's pet name for himself. I'm pretty sure he came up with it after reading up on the Zuni—Native Americans from the Zuni River Valley in New Mexico, a place he loved to visit. Zuni fetishes are small carvings depicting animals and icons integral to their culture. An owl represents wisdom and truth and is an animal that sees things that others may not.

I got sick to my stomach when I started reading the comment. He posted something about my forecast and used my childhood nickname, "Pookie," so I knew it was from him.

I was surprised and a little weirded out that he decided to get in touch on my weather blog. I deleted his message right away on the Foxnews.com site, but I emailed him back at the address I had from several years ago:

Hey Dad

It's taken me a while to write. I wasn't sure I was going to since it's been so long, and I was a little shocked to see you responding to a blog I wrote. I guess I figured if you wanted to get in touch, there were other ways to go about it.

I'm not mad—or sad—or feel anything. I find it a little bizarre that you chose my work blog to say hello—or to leave a cryptic message so that I would know you were out there.

Obviously, I'm glad you're alive—and I guess back in Canada. Last I heard you were in Nebraska. I forwarded your email to Craig as well to see if he wanted to get in touch. Not sure if he has or not.

So, I guess you knew I was at Fox. I left after a year with Imus. They treat me well here. I enjoy what I do and the people I work with. I just finished my courses to become a meteorologist and am waiting for my AMS seal of approval. I got married in June to a wonderful person. We live in Manhattan, and it feels like home here.

Anyhow, I'm not sure what your motivation was for writing. If you want to send a note, this is my email address.

Janice

He wrote a lengthy email back to me as if nothing had ever happened. He explained that by responding to my Fox weather blog he was trying to make contact as "simply" as possible. He never wanted to be out of contact with me or Craig—and it was kind of our fault, because we had his email address. He reasoned we could have gotten in touch whenever we wanted. He felt we were happy, doing fine, and busy with our lives.

There were comments on my job with Imus: he had watched me every day and couldn't believe I had lasted that long. Then he talked about how he saw my weather updates on Fox, filling in for various anchors, and that my progress and growth at the company was amazing! He saw I was married to "Shaun" and he seemed like a great guy.

Several paragraphs were dedicated to his career winding down, and how he had written a book that had done well in British Columbia. There were several moves back and forth from Canada to the US and then some health issues with acute rheumatoid arthritis. Along the way he talked about how he had helped his new wife's aunt, mom, and brother's eldest daughter. What a stand-up guy he was! He also detailed a massive heart attack that he wasn't expected to survive. Incredibly, he believed the medications he was on had cured his rheumatoid arthritis. Now he was retired, very happy, and thankful for every healthy and enjoyable day. The email ended saying he followed my career and read my blog all the time. He told me he loved me and my brother from the day we were born and that would never change no matter what. "Would you like our address? Or maybe just exchange emails? You can forward this to Craig (is he still in Toronto?) if you like. Love, Dad."

This was one of the weirdest things I've ever experienced: getting this update from my father. But he had given me some important information too. The fact that my dad had severe rheumatoid arthritis was helpful, because it's in the same family as multiple sclerosis. They are both autoimmune diseases and both result when something misfires in your immune system. And now I knew I had to write possible heart issues in my family history when I filled out doctors' forms.

We then exchanged a few more emails, which I have reread while writing this chapter. They are extremely painful and hurtful—on both sides. At the time, I was bitter and upset, and blamed him for a lot. He wrote back with some awful stuff, too, and none of it resolved anything. I was angry. He was defensive.

I later found out that my mom had tried to contact my dad, writing him and calling him after my terrifying home invasion in Houston. She wanted him to know something terrible had happened to me and that he needed to get in touch. She also admitted that his new wife had emailed her saying mean things. Mom tearfully told me there were things she would never share because they were too painful to talk about.

My mother also tried to contact Dad when I was diagnosed with MS, yet he never reached out despite having my phone number and email. I was mad all over again. I wanted nothing to do with him. I couldn't believe he had been my hero when I was a kid. Who was this guy who just decided to up and leave his family and never stay in touch with his children? Why wouldn't he reach out after finding out I had been diagnosed with an incurable illness? He certainly had no problem taking care of his wife's extended family. And the assault in Houston: he knew. I needed him then more than I ever had in my whole life.

I asked my therapist, Judy, if it was okay to stop trying to have a relationship with him. She said if it caused too much pain, and it wasn't healthy for me, then, yes, it was okay to let him go.

Chapter 12

THE RETURN OF THE
GREEN SWEATER

Sean and I met in December of 2003, and he proposed in February of 2007. Sean admits that he should've proposed to me a lot sooner. I would have to agree. We both had busy lives and figured marriage would eventually happen. The main reason we wish we had gotten married earlier was to have kids a little sooner. However, there's a reason for everything, as they say. Sean did plan on proposing on a trip to Arizona the previous fall, but the ring he picked out wasn't ready. I was positive he was going to ask on that trip, and the night before we were leaving after a romantic week we got in one of the biggest fights of our relationship because I was so disappointed he hadn't asked me to marry him. He didn't tell me until months later, after he finally did propose, that he got the call that the engagement ring wasn't ready when we were at the airport and about to leave. He didn't want to do it without the diamond he had picked and the ring he had made. The jeweler had told him afterward that he could've FedEx'd the ring to the hotel in Arizona—they do it all the time (with a massive insurance policy, mind you). But that was after he finally proposed. All was forgiven.

One day while we were both in the middle of studying for big exams—for me it was my meteorology courses and him for his captain's test—he told me we should both take a break and go for breakfast. We were living together near Central Park on West Eighty-Second Street and he suggested we take a walk through the park. He came out of the bedroom wearing the sweater he had worn on our very first date. I remember it was a moss-green wool sweater that had a Christmasy pattern on it. I would see it from time to time in the closet and tell him he should wear it more often. I don't think he ever did wear it again until this one morning when he announced we should go out for breakfast.

I was so overwhelmed with work and studying that I didn't think about the reason why he decided to take the green wool sweater out of storage. I think I just probably looked at him and was disturbed that he was still trim enough to wear a sweater that was over five years old.

I remember being grumpy that morning because of my workload, but the fresh air was helping. I asked him: Where did he want to go, and why the hell were we walking so much to get a bacon and egg on a roll? He thought maybe we should check out our old restaurant Prime Burger, since we hadn't been there in so long.

I was hungry enough that I didn't care at that point. (I was still not clueing in to these hints he was dropping.) When we finally got to the restaurant, I was starving. We were about to walk in, when we realized the lights weren't on and the sign said CLOSED. I had forgotten it was Sunday. Damn! A couple of female tourists walked by and stopped where we were standing under some scaffolding.

"Is this the famous restaurant where that *Sex and the City* episode was filmed?" they asked me.

"Yes," I said. "But it's closed!"

"Darn! We were hoping to see the place!"

I told my newfound friends that this was the spot my boyfriend and I had our first date. We were going to have breakfast there, until this terrible development with the CLOSED sign.

The tourists said they knew another restaurant up the street that they had heard was decent.

"Good. We're coming with you," I said.

Sean grabbed my arm. He looked a little spooked.

"No, wait a minute," he said.

My new girlfriends were already ten paces ahead of us.

"Sean! I'm starving! Let's find another place! Let's follow them!"

"No. Wait." He reached into his breast pocket.

What? What is he doing? I wondered. *Why is he reaching into his pocket? No. Is this happening? Is this really happening?*

Immediately my brain was going over everything that had happened up to this moment. The sweater. The long walk. The Prime Burger.

My heart.

Sean opened the square velvet-covered box, and I saw a little sparkle.

"Will you marry me?"

OH, MY GOD.

"Of course I will."

Predictably, I cried. Sean knew I would, so he brought out his handkerchief from the same pocket.

In front of the Prime Burger where we had had our first date, beneath the scaffolding only steps away from St. Patrick's Cathedral, I became the luckiest girl in the world.

So many things had to happen for Sean and me to find each other. Lianne and Tony had to get married. I had to move back to Ottawa and then to New York. Sean had to fulfill a lifelong dream by going surfing in Hawaii after 9/11, and the weather had to create those gigantic waves so he couldn't surf that day, and instead decided to climb a mountain.

In a lot of ways, we had both lost our footing at times or gotten tired along our trek to find each other, but we got to the top. And then the sun came out.

Jumping ahead ten years, in the spring of 2017, Sean and I were in our living room catching up on each other's busy day after putting the kids to bed. We were going over the highlights of our week—what was going on at the office, our boys' lives at school, the funny things they said or did, our summer plans—when Sean looked at me and said somewhat seriously: "We have a big anniversary coming up."

My mind went into alert mode. Anniversary? What day was it? What month were we in? Life was speeding by in a colorful blur, and I felt like I had to take a moment and slow my brain down. Wedding anniversary? Wait, how long had we been married? Quick math. Finger counting. Wow. Ten years.

I thought about it for a moment. So much had happened, and yet it seemed like only yesterday that we were planning to spend the rest of our lives together. When Sean and I got engaged, in 2007, we thought about having a wedding, but we were both so busy. He was studying to become a captain; I was trying to get all my courses done to be a broadcast meteorologist. We started writing down a guest list. Trying to figure out the how, what, where. We were stressed-out. My family was in Canada. Who would we invite? We didn't have a lot of money to put something together, and we didn't want to hurt the feelings of family members and friends who never got an invitation. Then one of us had an idea: *Why don't we elope? Pick a day on the calendar and go to City Hall?* That sounded like a perfect plan. I bought a dress; he bought a suit. We had our friends Mark and Jen stand up for us, and we both took the day off work. It was a beautiful June day.

Sean asked me if, on our tenth anniversary, we could get married in a church.

"Make it official?" I laughed.

Our boys would be there with us. How special to have our two most cherished gifts from our union to share in our wedding vows. I wouldn't want it any other way. We loved a beautiful Catholic church that was in our old parish on the Upper West Side called Holy Trinity. We knew the priest there, Father Gary Mead, who had baptized Theodore, so we met with him to ask if he could perform the ceremony. We weren't looking for a big wedding, just a renewal of vows with some close friends. It was Father Gary who suggested we do it all, "from soup to nuts," including a singer and an organist. He would be honored to be included.

We had about two dozen people attending. All the kids of our friends and family took part as flower girls and altar boys. Sean hired a party bus to take us from our house to the church and then to the reception. The pictures conveyed pure joy. The weather, just like the day, was perfect.

Looking back on my life, I've come to realize that my marriage to Sean was the best thing that ever happened to me. For so many years I was on my own and wondered if I would ever find a partner to share my life with. When I trace my steps, I see every path I've gone down—every job I've taken, every city I've lived in and the experiences I've had—has led me to meeting this person. He's the best man I know. We still enjoy each other's company, laugh easily together, share the same values, and are so blessed to have our beautiful boys. I cannot imagine my life without him.

A couple of years ago, when we were back in Ottawa for Christmas, we took Matthew and Theodore to meet Lianne and Tony. We all had breakfast together in their home as our kids played with their daughter in the living room. We realized it had been fifteen years since their honeymoon and their hike when they met Sean. We took a picture before we left. I put it next to the photo they had taken fifteen years ago in Hawaii. Lianne tells me it's her favorite story of all time to tell people. I tell her she's the world's greatest matchmaker.

Someday, Sean says he wants to take our family hiking on the same trail where he found Lianne and Tony—and then eventually found me. To tell them the story. Of how they came to be. And the mountains we both had to climb to find each other.

Chapter 13

YOU ARE MY SUNSHINE: MATTHEW AND THEODORE

Motherhood changed my life; it may have even saved it.

I remember the day that Sean and I decided to seriously think about having kids. It was during a trip to my neurologist's office. How romantic!

We were sitting with Dr. Tullman, going over my latest MRI results. He looked up at us and said:

"Are you guys thinking of having children?"

I was a little taken aback and looked at Sean and then back at Dr. Tullman. I noticed there were pictures of his family all over his office.

"Well, we've talked about it a little . . ."

Again I looked at Sean, who was just sitting quietly, staring ahead.

Dr. Tullman smiled, gently turned a picture of his family our way, and said kids are amazing. He had two of them himself. Then he described how pregnancy for women living with MS could be life-changing. Back when we didn't know much about the illness, women were told to avoid getting pregnant because it might make their MS worse. After decades of research and studies, the conclusion is the opposite. Pregnancy reduces the number of MS relapses, especially in the second and third trimester.

My eyes widened.

"Can I go off the meds?"

"Yes, while you are trying to get pregnant you may go off the injections. And then you can forget about them during pregnancy . . . and if you breastfeed."

I looked at Sean. And smiled. I think I might've said:

"When can we get started?"

After that visit, Sean and I began talking about babies very seriously. I started to let my imagination about being a mom run free. We decided to give it a try. We also agreed that if it wasn't meant to be, then we wouldn't push it. In other words, I was thirty-seven at the time and knew my age could potentially make it harder to have kids. We wanted to do it naturally, without any medical intervention. When I look back at those days when we both realized we wanted to try, it's like sunshine burst through the clouds.

While we were trying, I also started researching MS and pregnancy. I asked Dr. Tullman if there was a chance I could pass MS along to my kids. He told me it's not a directly inherited disease, so there's not a single gene that passes on MS. MS is thought to occur as a result of a combination of genetic factors. I had learned that my father had acute rheumatoid arthritis, also an autoimmune condition, so that could've been part of the reason I was predisposed. Researchers are also looking at the correlation between environmental and immune factors. It's also worth noting that in Canada, people have a greater risk of developing MS than any other country. Scientists think it could be the fact that there's not enough sunlight to help with vitamin D production. Or it could be more exposure to viruses or a genetic predisposition.

The MS Society of Canada even had a campaign a few years back branding MS as Canada's disease based on the data that the country is home to the world's highest incidence of multiple sclerosis. There were billboards up that read: WORLD LEADER IN HOCKEY, MAPLE SYRUP, AND MS.

Not exactly the most uplifting poster to read while you're waiting for the bus.

I was encouraged by the articles I was seeing about MS in pregnancy. Having the disease doesn't harm the baby. In fact, it's the other way around. Studies show that, in many pregnancies, patients IMPROVE. After having both my kids, I went years without any new symptoms or lesions. I even asked Dr. Tullman if there was a chance having kids slowed the progression of the illness. There is a significant drop in relapse rates, especially during the second and third trimesters, with up to an 80 percent reduction in the third trimester.

It's almost like our immune systems stop going crazy, and everything in our bodies works together to protect the baby.

I've talked to many women who have MS and said during their pregnancies they felt amazing, with much more energy than usual. One of the most common symptoms is fatigue, and so many of us get a break from that sense of always being tired, and even the sensory and cognitive issues like numbness and tingling go away.

According to the National Multiple Sclerosis Society, there are two main theories for why pregnancy helps with MS symptoms. For starters, pregnancy leads to a shift in immune responses. You're carrying a baby that has half foreign DNA from the father, so your immune system has to change in a way that makes your body less likely to reject the fetus.

The other theory focuses on the anti-inflammatory and seemingly "neuroprotective power" of pregnancy hormones.

This isn't to say that all women who have MS have easy pregnancies, of course, but the benefits certainly outweigh the negatives.

So, with all this awesome information I was receiving—plus the fact that I could stop with the daily injections—Project Babymaking began.

I recently stumbled on a diary entry I wrote the day I found out I was pregnant. I smiled when I read it, because like a virtual time machine, it took me right back . . .

Saturday, May 24th, 2008

Today was the day (yelling this at the top of my lungs) I found out I was pregnant! I can't tell you what kind of emotional roller coaster ride I've been on for the last 6 hours.

I've been tired and kind of "under the weather" for the last few weeks . . . Falling asleep much earlier than usual at night and sleeping for 8–9 hours . . . little hot flashes during the day and feeling flushed . . . a little dizzier than usual, out of breath . . . The week before this past one I was craving fruit salad at night for several nights, which is weird for me.

This morning (Saturday) I woke up at 5 a.m. and decided I was going to take a pregnancy test since things were a little "off schedule" . . .

Once I got it in my head that being pregnant could be a possibility, I could not stop my brain from going crazy . . . like what if I'm pregnant? What is it going to be like being pregnant . . . what kind of mother will I be . . . how much weight will I gain!! (Eek!)

I made myself a coffee (we're allowed 1–2 cups a day according to the Internet . . . just in case I really am pregnant) . . . and took a vitamin (with the recommended dose of folic acid . . . just in case . . .) and then put on my sneakers (still in my pajamas with a coat on top—I love New York) and set out to the 24 hour Duane Reade [pharmacy] to pick up my pregnancy kit. (Besides, we needed soap and toilet paper anyway. Might as well pick up a pregnancy test while I'm there, right?)

It took me ten minutes to find the actual pregnancy test aisle once I got to Duane Reade. (It was about 5:35 a.m. by this time.) Once I got there, though, I was in EPT hell. There were about 15 brands to choose from . . . I decided I was going to go for the easiest one to find out the result . . . the 25 dollar "digital" test that had an extra one included "just to make sure!" And I threw in a gigantic bag of M&M's as well . . . M&M's and an EPT test . . . hmmm . . . what did I need a pregnancy test for?

I got to the cash register and said "GOOD MORNING!" a little too loudly for the clerk. I had a feeling he's seen this kind of thing before—5 a.m. pregnancy tests.

Walking home I started doing the math. If I AM pregnant, then when would this baby arrive? Sometime in January.

I get home, tear my jacket off, and try to read the directions of the pregnancy test . . . okay easy enough—pee on a stick. And wait . . . wait . . . wait . . . (thinking about how I forgot to get toilet paper and soap at the store . . .)

It was the longest three minutes of my life.

Finally . . .

PREGNANT

I can't believe it. Is this for real? What the?????? How did this happen? Oh yeah—5th-grade health class . . . I decide I can't wait to tell my husband. I must go wake him . . . I rush in . . . he somehow senses I'm in the room staring at him TO WAKE UP and opens his eyes. He asks if I'm coming back to bed. It's too early to be up.

I crawl inside and tell him I have news. He's wide-awake in a split second.

"I'm pregnant." Heartbeat . . . heartbeat . . .

"Oh my . . . wow . . . oh . . ."

It was good, though. I could tell he was happy (a little shocked and maybe feeling like he was still in a dream sequence).

We got up—kept looking at one another . . . I kept asking him how he felt . . . and how crazy this is . . .

As he made me pancakes (my favorite—and this was a special pancake occasion) . . . we kept looking at each other, trying to figure out what the other one was thinking . . . and said we couldn't believe it could happen this fast . . . I think I'm still in shock. It's now 1 p.m., and after going for a long walk and a quick trip into Barnes and Noble to buy 3 "what to expect when you're expecting" type books to read, I'm writing this out now. I want to remember this day. I want to remember what it was like to see the "pregnant" stick and the look on my husband's face . . . and to venture for the very first time into the "expecting mothers" aisle at Barnes and Noble.

I'm shocked, happy, scared, insecure, blessed, and wondering how the next 9 months are going to go . . . and how on earth I will take care of a small, little person? I guess we're about to find out!

The first trimester was tough. I had to take a week off from work because I was so ill from morning sickness. I tried everything, from motion sickness bracelets to acupuncture. I was never physically sick, just had a constant state of nausea. I was also having mini-anxiety attacks on air. I remember one time specifically I was in the studio with Megyn Kelly and Bill Hemmer during the 9:00 a.m.

show *America's Newsroom*. I was doing my weather report, and I had trouble catching my breath. I had to stop in the middle of the forecast. Bill and Megyn knew there was something wrong, so they jumped in:

"Thanks for that report, JD. In other news . . ."

I was mortified. It goes down as one of my most embarrassing moments on air. There are times of course where I get nervous, and I get "breathy" sometimes, but this was full-blown anxiety. Tom Lowell, the senior producer, got in my earpiece and asked if I was okay. I was near tears. I didn't know what to say. I just said I didn't feel well. I ran upstairs to my office and started to cry. I ended up telling Megyn that I was pregnant, and of course, she was thrilled for me. I was hoping I could get through the next five months.

My therapist, Judy, thinks that the fact that I was pregnant and perhaps more self-conscious than usual led to the anxiety. It felt like the whole world was watching my changing body on a day-to-day basis and it was a little unsettling.

Some days I could get through my weather reports relatively smoothly, but there were other times I struggled. I had the same thing happen to me when I was pregnant with Theodore. My friends and coworkers Jon Scott and Jenna Lee guessed I was having a baby before the official announcement. They both noticed my shortness of breath while I was reporting. As much as being pregnant is miraculous, it is additionally very stressful.

I also learned during this time that chivalry is dead in the New York City transit system. More women got up to give me their seats in crowded trains than men did. I would catch them looking at my pregnant belly and then pretend to read or close their eyes so they didn't have to get up. This was when I was eight or nine months pregnant—so no excuse that they didn't know I was standing for two. I had to chuckle when there was an actual campaign in New York on subway etiquette, including a drawing of someone giving their seat to a pregnant lady or the elderly. My husband has always been a perfect gentleman, and this kind of behavior has always come naturally to him. I thank his parents, Mickey and Dee, for raising such a good, polite, offer-your-seat-to-the-pregnant-lady person.

Even before the social media revolution, I would sometimes get rude emails from viewers asking me when I was having that baby so they could finally see their hometown on the weather map my huge belly was blocking!

When I was pregnant with Theodore, I wanted to do something fun when announcing my pregnancy on the air. With Matthew, I just turned sideways and had my friend Jane Skinner play along with me. This time around I thought it would be cute to switch from a weather map to a sonogram to show that the "weather machine" was now the "baby machine."

Soon afterward I got a call from the VP of programming.

"I'm all for pregnant ladies on TV, but I don't need to see a sonogram of their fetus in my face."

So that wasn't fun feedback. By the way, since then, I have seen many sonograms on our air. Perhaps he had something against baby weather maps.

I remember one day I was walking down the hallway and a female on-air talent who had three children herself decided to joke:

"BEEP BEEP BEEP BEEP! Everybody back up! The WIDE LOAD is coming through!" Like I was a truck backing up. I was in tears. This was in front of dozens of people, including coworkers and *Fox & Friends* guests in the greenroom.

Just because we're pregnant doesn't mean we don't have feelings and are immune to fat jokes.

Near the end of both of my pregnancies, everything was hard: sleeping, standing, sitting, putting on clothes, walking, and breathing. Despite all of this, I was so excited to meet this new little person whose heart was beating next to mine.

Sean and I agreed we both wanted to know the sex of our babies early. (Well, I kinda agreed for both of us . . .) I've always been terrible about keeping or wanting to know secrets. Even as a young kid I would go searching all through my house before Christmas to find hidden presents. One year I carefully unwrapped a couple of gifts that were in my parents' closet when no one was home (sorry, Mom—and thank you for that Cabbage Patch doll!). I've also been known to give my kids presents before holidays or birthdays because I get so excited, I can't wait. When I had prenatal testing done, I said YES immediately both times to find out whether I was having a boy or a girl. Sean probably could've waited for the surprise, but since I was the one carrying, he didn't have a choice.

Matthew Stephen was born January 24, 2009. He was a planned C-section because he was a breech baby. I had checked in to the hospital with Sean in the morning. My wonderful OB-GYN, Dr. Waterstone, who delivered both my kids, was a welcome sight. Everything went smoothly before, during, and after delivery, including the lovely epidural that kept everything pain-free. My husband held my hand when Dr. Waterstone laid Matthew on my chest. And my life as a mom began.

As beautiful as being a mom is, the first few months were one of the biggest challenges I've ever had. I would even go as far as saying it was a very dark period. I was set on breastfeeding Matthew, but he never really liked it. I remember one day while in the hospital I was trying everything to get Matthew to latch on, so I was totally naked from the waist up, my hair was a greasy mess, my skin had broken out, and my boy was screaming at the top of his lungs as I tried to get him to feed. My gorgeous friend Jane Skinner came through the door to meet the baby in full Fox hair and makeup and a beautiful winter coat. Her face turned from smiles and excitement to surprise and perhaps—terror? God bless her, though. She could've turned around and walked right back out the door. I wouldn't have blamed her. This wasn't for the faint of heart. She just took off her coat and asked how she could help.

Matthew was not an easy baby. He was perhaps what some would call "colicky." He never slept longer than an hour or two. He never wanted to breastfeed. It was so hard to calm him down. Sean reminds me that friends and relatives thought we were crazy, but if you came to our apartment and spent an hour or two with Matthew, you would walk out shell-shocked. It was that hard. Sean and I had some of our biggest fights during this time. We were both sleep-deprived and frustrated. There were many nights that he would strap Matthew up in a BabyBjörn and circle the American Museum of Natural History at two in the morning. I thought it was so I could get rest. Sean politely says it was to take a little break from me. I appreciate the honesty.

During the days, I would bundle Matthew up every day to stroll around Central Park to get out of the apartment even if it was 10 degrees with a windchill below zero. I cried a lot. No one tells you how hard having a baby can be. I was scared to leave Matthew with anyone. We did hire a wonderful woman named Diana who was a doula to help with the breastfeeding and keep me sane. She was one of the only people I would let take Matthew so I could rest, or sometimes she would cook a meal.

My mom and brother came to visit, and I remember being a complete wreck. I didn't want anyone to stay with us or attempt to help.

When I look back, I know I had postpartum depression. I cried all the time and hardly left the apartment. I never left Matthew for more than fifteen minutes. His crib was right next to our bed, but most of the time he would end up sleeping with us, because we were so exhausted from picking him up.

I was always with him, trying to soothe him or feed him or get him to sleep. Diana the doula had recommended getting an exercise ball and bouncing Matthew on it while swaddled to help him sleep. I was bouncing on that ball constantly. My abs were probably in better shape after pregnancy than they had ever been my whole life.

When researching MS and pregnancy, I came upon some interesting information. Depression and anxiety are twice as common among people living with MS. So it stands to reason that postpartum depression might also be common.

I always tell new moms that it's normal to feel helpless and sometimes a failure when you're trying to do all of this. Try to ask for help. I wish I had just let people help me more.

I took off the whole four months of work I was given at Fox. Because Matthew was never comfortable breastfeeding, I would pump every few hours and feed him from a bottle. That gave us all of the work of breastfeeding with none of the convenience. He was later diagnosed with reflux, and we eventually got him on the right medicine.

Someone recommended I join a mommy group to get out of the apartment more. I went to one lunch but was so terrified Matthew would cry the whole time, I never went again. I did meet one mom named Amy whose name I somehow managed to type into my Black-Berry. She was in her late thirties, too, and had a boy named Will about the same age as Matthew. Amy was someone I leaned on and did playdates with in the park. I remember one day we were both attempting to breastfeed in Central Park with our Hooter Hiders (a code name for the piece of fabric that you drape across your chest while feeding your child). We were both trying to unfasten our layers of winter clothes on a park bench when two other women speed walking on a trail in front of us said loud enough for us to hear, "I remember those days. AND I DON'T MISS THEM ONE BIT."

Amy and I looked at each other with our tired faces with semi-permanent dark circles under our eyes and scowled. "Bitches."

I recently did a feature for *Fox & Friends* about being a mom and advice I would give to new mommies. Many of my fellow mothers talked about sleep training as something that helped them. I could never leave either of my kids crying for more than a minute. My heart hurt too much. I'm not saying this is right, and I am in awe of parents who can get their kids to put themselves to sleep. But now, at ages eight and ten, my kids sleep soundly through the night, although part of me misses them coming into our bed. I always say to new moms: Take everyone's advice on how to raise your children with a grain of salt. You and your husband will do what you think is best. I remember one close relative saying, "You are not doing anyone any favors by having your child with you in your bedroom. And why are you still breastfeeding when you have MS? You're going to have another relapse." My relationship with that person has never been the same since her motherly recommendations. Many people, from friends to relatives to complete strangers, will try to give you advice. They all think, incorrectly, that your baby might be like their baby. Just do your best, and you'll find your way.

As my four-month maternity leave was coming to an end, Sean and I had to figure out what we were going to do for child care. There was a day care close to Fox that we registered Matthew for, but because he was so fussy and upset all the time, I thought maybe we should have just one person take care of him. I started emailing all my mommy friends at work to see if they knew of any nannies whom they would recommend. This would be expensive for us, I realized, but I wanted Matthew to get one-on-one care while Sean and I were working. This prospect gave me even more anxiety as my days going back to work were getting nearer.

I decided to reach out to my little built-in network of mamas at

Fox who might be able to help. My friend and former colleague Alisyn Camerota came to the rescue.

Alisyn's nanny knew of someone named DebiAn who came highly recommended and lived in the city. I called her, and she agreed to come for an interview. I thank God for the day DebiAn came through our apartment door. She was a tall, kind Jamaican woman who had an easy laugh and a wide, welcoming smile. As soon as she sat down, she asked to see Matthew. He was in his crib, just waking up. I took her into the bedroom and she picked him up. He didn't cry. I asked her a few questions about her background and her job experience, but, honestly, the fact that she just wanted to come and meet Matthew? I knew she was our nanny.

From that day forward, DebiAn has been with us. She is part of our family. Our kids adore her. She is one of the main reasons why they are smart, sweet, well-behaved boys. I am forever grateful to Alisyn for connecting me to DebiAn.

There are many books and articles written about how to "have it all" by being a career woman while raising a family. The reason I can do it is quite simply because I have help. From neighbors to friends to DebiAn and family. It takes a village. My boys are incredibly lucky that they have so many people who love and care for them. "Having it all" means different things to different moms. For me it's doing a job I love with a supportive husband and a network of people who are there to lend a hand. I have friends and neighbors who have all chipped in at one point or another, and I enjoy helping out with hosting playdates, carpooling, and being part of a neighborhood mommy network.

Heading back to work after four months off with Matthew was terrifying. Once I got back into the swing of things, I started to enjoy myself again. I had part of my old life back. I could chat with friends without having an ear out for a crying baby, and after months of not brushing my hair or wearing makeup, it was nice to feel a bit more put together. One more thing I mention to moms is to not feel guilty or beat yourself up for feeling happy at work and away from your kids for a while. It's okay to miss them and feel sad about not being home as well. It's all normal. I find that after being at the office all day, when I get home and I get to see my boys, they've got the best of me because I am so grateful to see them and hear about their day.

I pumped breast milk for close to a year with Matthew and was able to freeze extra while I was at home. Looking back now, I was a little too obsessed with the breast milk situation. I did the same with Theodore, although it was easier to breastfeed with my second baby. Theodore didn't have the same issues with latching on or feeding. I was able to store a freezer full of breast milk with both of them. (Many moms call it liquid gold because of the antibodies that help your baby fight off viruses and bacteria. It also lowers your baby's risk of having asthma or allergies. Plus, babies who are breast-fed exclusively—without any formula—for the first six months have fewer ear infections, respiratory illnesses, and bouts of diarrhea!)

Yes, I was obsessed. So obsessed that when Hurricane Irene was forecast to make landfall across the Northeast with the possibility of power outages, I kept harassing Sean to buy a generator. Not be-cause of the usual reasons to buy a generator for warmth or keeping the appliances running, but because I COULDN'T LOSE ALL OF THE LIQUID GOLD I HAD PUMPED ALL OF THOSE MONTHS! I started imagining all that milk going bad and losing my mind. I would wake up in a cold sweat thinking there was a chance I would lose precious ounces of my hard-earned pumping. Thankfully we didn't lose power. We now have a generator, which we eventually used during Hurricane Sandy a year later.

Once I was back at work—Matthew was beginning to grow out of his colic/reflux stages, and Sean and I were starting to get more sleep—we decided to throw a wrench into the normalcy and try to get pregnant again. I was thirty-eight, and I knew the fertility window was closing rapidly. I had been lucky with Matthew, but if we were going to try and have a second, we needed to get back on the baby train.

I got pregnant again quickly. I didn't even need a pregnancy test. My makeup artist knew right away just by my skin and my mood. I took a real test after she gave her accurate diagnosis and told Sean my good news. We had already started to tell friends and family, when one morning I woke up and felt cramping. I started spotting and knew something was wrong. I called my OB-GYN's office and let them know what was going on. They had me come in right away. There was something different with this pregnancy. I tried to anticipate the possibility of bad news, but you can never prepare yourself when your doctor tries to listen for a heartbeat that you heard just a week ago but is now no longer registering.

"I'm sorry, Janice," said Dr. Waterstone. "You did nothing that caused this miscarriage, and there is absolutely nothing you could have done differently. It's not your fault."

You're sitting there in a cold doctor's office in your hospital gown, looking down at your socks, and it's hard not to cry.

Dr. Waterstone tells me it's going to be okay. You'll try again. She reminds me that half of miscarriages are because of chromosomal abnormalities—that the baby wouldn't, couldn't, survive. Nature takes over.

I called Sean as soon as I got out of the doctor's office. "It didn't make it. There's no heartbeat."

"I'm sorry, Mama." There was a long silence. I know it's because Sean didn't quite know what to say. What can you say over the phone? He wasn't expecting the doctor's visit to go like this.

"Just go and see Matthew. I'm coming home," he said.

I went home and hugged my beautiful Matthew. We were lucky we had this little boy. I wasn't sure I was ready to go through this again.

Dr. Waterstone told me that after a miscarriage when you have your first full period, it's the best time to try again. It's almost like the body still thinks it's pregnant and wants to have a baby in there. So Sean and I followed her advice. This time I was in full fertility mode, taking my body temperature, and I had bought a device that when I peed on a stick and stuck it into a little portable machine, it would tell me if I was ovulating. We were visiting Fox News anchor Jon Scott's beautiful vacation home with Matthew when I found out I was pregnant again. (Not sure if I ever mentioned this to Jon Scott in person. So. Jon Scott, if you're reading this, thank you for the good luck!)

I felt the familiar morning sickness—all day long—and shortness of breath I had with Matthew. It hadn't taken long for my body to return to pregnancy mode.

We went through the tests early to see if the baby was healthy and found out we were having another boy. We were thrilled. Matthew would be a wonderful big brother.

I didn't stress out as much with this pregnancy because I already knew what was going to happen week by week. With Matthew I had pretty much memorized *What to Expect When You're Expecting*. Because I wasn't as anxious, it was an easier pregnancy. The one thing that I remember was the strange guilt I was feeling about having another baby. How could I possibly love another son as much as I loved Matthew? I almost felt like I was betraying him somehow. As I was getting closer to my due date with his brother, I would cry at night because I worried about Matthew's feelings with a new baby competing for attention. Strange, I know, but I've since learned that many moms feel this way.

My good friend Megyn Kelly gave me a smart piece of advice. She told me to write Matthew a letter explaining to him how special he was. Your first child is an incredible gift. Write your feelings down for him so that he has it for the rest of his life.

The night before Theodore was born, I wrote Matthew a love letter. I still have it sealed with his name on it. I will give it to him when he's older to show him how special he is. I cried the whole time I was writing it.

At the moment his brother came into the world, my heart was fuller, and I had enough love for both of these beautiful, miraculous boys.

As I write this, I am sitting in the living room as they watch a movie huddled together under a blanket. They are the best of buddies, the two of them. When one of them is not around, they count the minutes until the other gets home. If one of them is upset about something, the other one starts to cry because they feel each other's pain. Yes, they argue and fight, but there is no doubt they are each other's best friend. I imagine them growing up and still being this close. They are two halves of their mama's heart.

I had Theodore Patrick on February 9, 2011. I was two months shy of my forty-first birthday. Sean and I tried one more time to have another child shortly after Theodore was born, but I had another miscarriage. I woke up one morning and knew immediately something was wrong.

I was walking to the train station to get to work, and I noticed a dead baby bird that had fallen out of a tree. Tears came to my eyes. That tiny bird was a reminder that sometimes babies don't make it. Sometimes their mamas can't save them. Sometimes nature can be cruel.

I made another appointment with Dr. Waterstone.

She confirmed the heartbeat was gone.

Dr. Waterstone then suggested maybe we try another route to get pregnant instead of the old-fashioned way. In vitro fertilization was an option. But I shook my head and said no. We were probably done.

I called Sean to tell him the sad news. This time around he paused and said:

"Let's just be happy with what we have, Mama. I wish I had proposed to you sooner, so we could've had many more babies. But I can't bear to see you go through another miscarriage. Let's just be grateful for our little miracles, Matthew and Theodore."

That was enough for me. Our wonderful family. The reason Sean and I were meant to meet. To bring these beautiful children into the world.

It's hard to put into words how two little people can bring such joy and love into our lives. It's like my life before them had been somewhat meaningless. I know many couples that don't have children, and they are happy and fulfilled. However, when I snuggle up with my sons at night, smell their hair, and talk about their day with them, I am at peace. Nothing else matters.

Sometimes Sean and I will stand over them while they sleep at night and whisper to each other while we watch them breathe:

"We created them. How did we make such handsome, funny, smart boys?"

I believe in God and was raised Catholic, but it's my children who make me believe there is something bigger out there than all of us.

They are pure sunshine. Sunshine that Sean and I made together.

Chapter 14

ONE FINAL MESSAGE

One morning a few weeks after my youngest son, Theodore, was born in 2011, I posted a baby picture on my weather blog. It was an adorable photo of Teddy grinning from ear to ear, wearing a little blue onesie. The title on the blog was "Cute Break."

It said:

Hi guys! Wanted to post this cute picture of Theodore I caught on my cell phone the other day. He's really starting to smile now! Too cute, right? Hope you're all doing well. Thanks for all the kind comments. I've got a little less than two months of maternity leave left. I'll be back just in time for the beginning of Hurricane Season! Talk to you soon.

I looked at the comments, and from out of the blue saw a note from Dad, "Zin owl." It said:

"He looks just like Matthew when he was born. Congratulations."

I hadn't talked with or emailed him for several years after our final falling-out. He never reached out after I had Matthew. And yet, he knew what Matthew looked like by following my blog and watching my life on the Fox News Channel. I wondered why he was cryptically contacting me again on a public forum. This time, I didn't respond.

That was March 30. He died a few weeks later.

The day before my birthday on May 8, I got an email from his wife—whom I had never met or talked to before.

It was titled "Hard News" and was addressed to me and my brother, Craig.

She said she was sorry the news had to come in an email. That there was no easy way to tell us, but Howard passed away in the hospital in Trail, British Columbia, where they lived. She wrote that he had had medical issues over the years, but this was something new. He went to the ER and they thought it was gallstones. They admitted him and began running tests. A few days later he was weak and the doctors realized he had end-stage cancer in the liver, stomach, and lungs.

He chose not to undergo treatment, which doctors admitted would not be successful. My dad lapsed into a coma and died on May 5.

She mentioned he loved us and was confident we were happy and enjoying life.

He would be cremated, with no funeral. She would scatter his ashes in the mountains.

I forwarded the email to my brother, Craig. And then I called him. He was sad, of course. But we were also so confused and hurt. So many years of not having contact with our dad. And then one day finding out he was gone. In an email.

I often think: *If I could change things, would I?* While I was trying to find pictures of my dad for this book, Matthew noticed an old family photo. He asked if that was his grandpa Howard. I put my arms around him and said yes. He began to cry and said, "I wish I could've met him. Why couldn't I meet him? It's not fair. I think I would love him." I broke down as well. Theodore then came in and saw we were both weeping and his tears began. Sean was out in the living room and wanted us to have a moment together. I told them their grandfather would've thought they were the best things in the whole world. In my heart, I see him looking over us and smiling. These boys are part of him too. But my one wish would be that they could've met him. Or at least he could've seen them and held them both in his arms before he died. I know he would think they were absolutely amazing. My mom tells the story of how Dad believed as humans we are made up of energy. When we are born, we are given that energy from our parents through birth. When we die, that energy leaves our body and becomes part of the universe again, like the stars that we see at night.

My brother, Craig, at the age of seven consoled one of his friends whose uncle had suddenly passed away. My mom overheard these two young boys talking about death, and my brother told his buddy my dad's "energy" story to help him through it. He told him all he had to do to see his uncle was look up at the sky and see the twinkling stars.

I read something the other day that made me think of that story— that family is like the stars in the sky. We don't have to see them all the time, but we know they are always there.

There's no question my dad had one of the biggest impacts on me early in life. Before I met Sean, I used to think happiness and success were wrapped up in a satisfying, long-lasting career. I grew up seeing my dad happiest when he was working. I remember him telling me not only to "find what you most love to do and it won't seem like work" but also that a good career would outlast everything, including love and relationships. Now I realized that happiness, for me, can be sitting quietly on a bench with my husband, watching our boys running and laughing in the sunshine. Or reading a book to our boys at the end of the day, snuggled up in bed. Career is important, but I don't want "She was a fantastic TV personality" written as the lede in my obituary. I'd rather have "She was a wonderful mom and wife and a good human being." And because I try to live with a mostly sunny outlook, I will leave you with one of my favorite stories about my dad that comes from a slightly embarrassing situation.

One weekend I went to a wedding with a boyfriend in Brockville, Ontario. It was about an hour and a half away from Ottawa. I was in my twenties, and the boyfriend was driving us in his car. At the rehearsal dinner, my date got so drunk that he could barely speak. He spilled the chicken on my lap, and I was so upset I decided I didn't want to be there. I went back to the hotel and called home. My mom picked up the phone, and I asked to speak to Dad. I was crying.

"Dad, I'm at a wedding in Brockville. What's-his-name is drunk, and I need to get out of here."

My dad asked me what hotel I was at and told me he'd be there as soon as he could.

When he arrived, I got in the car. He had two Tim Hortons coffees and a couple of donuts ready for the drive home. I don't remember our conversation. I just remember he was true to his word. He would always come if I needed help. I just had to call and ask.

I also often imagine if I had called him—reached out—after the home invasion or being diagnosed with MS and asked if he could come, I believe he would have. I think if I had called him up and said: "Dad, I need you to be with me," I would've gotten through to him. He would have been there.

My father was a brilliant, complicated, flawed human being. As we all are to some extent. When I became a parent, I realized we just try our best with the experiences we've had as our guide. My boys will always know their grandpa Howard is out there, part of the universe. All they have to do to see him is look up at the sky and see the twinkling stars. He will be looking down at them, winking from above.

Chapter 15

MOTHER OF FROGS

When I first started at Fox News, back in 2004, John Kasich hosted a program on the weekends. He's now the governor of Ohio and was a presidential candidate. An impressive résumé, to be sure. For me, John Kasich was someone who sparked an idea that would become an important project for me, bringing me great confidence and inspiration when I began to think my career was coming to an end.

John was as kind as they come, always said hello, and would smile as soon as he saw you coming. One day when I was walking to my office, he was strolling down the hallway toward his, and we stopped and began to chat. He was promoting a new book, and I asked if he could sign one for me. He had one with him, magically produced a black Sharpie, and inscribed it to me. Governor Kasich looked up and said words that would change my life:

"Janice Dean. You need to write children's books about weather. My girls get so scared during a thunderstorm. I think it would help them understand why they happen."

If you could draw a lightbulb over my head and pull the little string to make it suddenly light up the room, that's what happened in those few minutes with John Kasich.

After our little hallway pitch, I started thinking about the idea. A lot.

I shared this fun concept with my friend and confidante Jane Skinner, who thought it was brilliant. She mentioned it would expand my "brand" as the "weather machine" and help kids and parents understand the weather. She also told me to keep my idea quiet so that no one would steal it!

I had no clue how I was going to do it, but it gave me that little fire in my belly that made me think it could be a fun little side project. I contacted my lawyer, Bob Barnett, who had helped me with my contracts at Fox and who also happens to be one of the biggest book agents in the world. I told him the idea, and right away he thought it was a good one. One thing about Bob: if your idea doesn't excite him, he'll tell you in about two seconds. If he thinks it has potential, he'll pull out all the stops and help you with it. Bob had a few contacts he could put me in touch with. Meanwhile, he told me to work on an outline.

I started with the idea of a little girl who was afraid of thunderstorms and how she would crawl into bed with her parents every time she heard the loud crackle and boom in the distance. Her dad would try to soothe her by explaining why the sky sounded so angry. Looking back, the story wasn't great, but the editors from HarperCollins kids' books still agreed to see me. I was so excited when I walked into their offices in midtown just a few blocks away from Fox. I felt like pinching myself. A real, famous publishing house where some of the greatest children's books of all time have been created. Ones that I read in school and have read out loud to both my children: *Charlotte's Web*, *Where the Wild Things Are*, *Goodnight Moon*, and *The Giving Tree*.

The other reason I was so happy was because I had just found out I was pregnant with Matthew, so I thought this was a sure sign that I was meant to write children's books! I imagined myself in a big, bright, sunny Pottery Barn–decorated kids' room with my perfect baby boy, reading him my brand-new children's book while I juggled my career as a meteorologist, author, mommy, and wife with perfect hair and makeup.

Toni and Kate from Harper were terrific. They sat me down and gave it to me straight: Writing children's books is HARD. It's more work than it looks like, for less money than you'd guess. However, they liked my idea of a kids' weather book, and—let's face it—I had a good platform to sell them. They asked me to figure out what age group I wanted to target and how much science I wanted to put into it. Toni and Kate suggested that a lot of successful kids' books have animals as main characters. They give kids a sense of stability in a changing world because animals change much less rapidly than we do. Animals are also multicultural; kids of all races and colors can relate to them. They can also do things that a child character might not be able to.

In other words, "Write us something different, and we'll take another look . . ."

I went home and tried again. I didn't exactly take their advice. This time I decided to write about Mother Nature and her big atmospheric kitchen . . . creating recipes for thunderstorms, tornadoes, and blizzards. As weather people, we talk a lot about the ingredients or environmental conditions required for different types of weather events. I worked hard on a story line that rhymed.

I didn't hear back from the ladies at HarperCollins right away. I emailed them a few times to get some feedback and kept feverishly checking my email. A few weeks went by, and I finally got an official "We're not interested at this time" letter in the mail. I was heartbroken.

Having talked to so many authors and illustrators since then, I know that these letters are commonplace. Many take pride in all their rejection letters. Dozens of famous authors have posted their "Thanks but no thanks" notes on publishing letterhead via social media. However, determined authors never give up. They get right back on the bike again and keep writing. I knew in my heart I had a great idea. At some point I would tackle it again.

It took a few years to figure it out, but I always had it in the back of my mind that this was a project I didn't want to give up on.

I started reading both of my boys a lot of children's books and taking mental notes on what I thought worked and didn't work. I began trying to come up with animals that might be fun characters to use to create a world of weather. When I first started at Fox, they called me a "Foxcaster" and my weather report was a "Foxcast," so I thought maybe I would steal that name and have a fox do weather. Then I thought that might be too close to home.

I remembered reading something about frogs being natural fore-casters. When frogs mate, they lay eggs in bodies of fresh water. Scientists have noticed that their mate-searching croaks occur right before the rain starts. They have an acute sense of how the atmo-sphere is changing, and if there are showers in the forecast, they can find a comfy place for the female frogs to lay eggs. Their croaking is a way to let their mates know their mood is about to get, ahem, amorous. I was onto something! Instead of a Foxcaster, what about a frogcaster? Sal Croaker would be a great name for a lead charac-ter! I then started doing a little more research on children's weather books. What was I up against? There were weather books out there that looked complicated, with lots of technical definitions and ex-planations that didn't look very kid-friendly. Then there were ones with very little detail, pictures showing wind blowing leaves around or rain falling from a cloud. There wasn't an "in-between" book that explained the science behind weather with a fun story that would appeal to kids. There was a void that could be filled.

I began to write an outline for a children's book about a frog who loved to forecast. I had no idea if the idea would work, but I wasn't going to give up on this. I told my friend Jane Skinner that I was going to try this children's weather book idea again at some point. She agreed it was too good not to keep trying.

Months went by, and I was still thinking about frogcasting ideas. I wanted the character to be female to encourage young girls to think about careers in science and math. We're still a minority in these fields. Fredricka the frog was the name I was thinking about— Freddie for short. I wrote the outline and saved it on my computer.

Then an unexpected interview with a well-known musician jumpstarted my children's book dreams once again.

Chuck Leavell is one of the most famous keyboardists in the world. He's worked with the Rolling Stones, Eric Clapton, the Allman Brothers, John Mayer, the Black Crowes—the list goes on. Not only is he a well-established artist, he is also a tree farmer and a cofounder of the website Mother Nature Network. Chuck has an avid interest in weather and the environment. When his people approached me about doing an interview with him, I leapt at the chance.

We got along very well. I told him about my classic rock background, and he asked about how I got into the business of doing the weather. He told me stories about being a tree farmer and how this was one of his most important missions in life. He even wrote a children's book about it. This perked up my ears, and I wanted to know more. I asked him how he had found a publisher and was able to get his idea on paper with an illustrator.

He mentioned that a friend of his had helped him with it, and it was a project of love. He never expected to make any money from it. He just thought it would be fun. I then told him about my idea about a weather-forecasting frog. He laughed and said he thought it was a good one. Without any prompting, he told me to send him my outline and he would read it and pass it along to his buddy in the publishing world.

I dusted off my Fredricka the Frogcaster outline and sent it to Chuck Leavell with a smile. You never know who is going to end up helping your dreams in this world. The keyboardist for the Rolling Stones sent my little story about a forecasting frog to his friend to see if he could lend a hand.

I got an email back quickly from Mr. Leavell, who told me his buddy would love to assist. It turns out his publishing connection was someone I had worked with indirectly named Peter Barnes. Peter worked at Fox Business, and even though we didn't see each other because he lived in DC, we certainly knew one another and had exchanged hellos through the years. It turns out Peter and his wife, Cheryl, were cofounders of a publishing company and both had written and illustrated children's books. Cheryl was now working with a publishing house in DC that was branching out into kids' books. They would be more than happy to look at my outline and pitch it for me.

From there, little Freddie came to life with a few changes. The biggest switch we made was Fredricka became a male character, since apparently it would be harder to sell a book about a female frog back then (today I'll bet they would've embraced Fredricka). Because our leading frog was a boy, I made sure Freddy was surrounded by female frogcasting role models. Sal Croaker turned into Sally Croaker, who was the chief frogcaster at the Frog News Network. Polly Woggins was the new, young, attractive frog who was starting out and was more interested in appearing on camera than making sure her forecasts were accurate. They all lived in Lilypad, where Freddy would work part-time after school in the frogcasting department.

I wrote the first book about a thunderstorm that was threatening

Me at four years old with my mother, father, and brother, Craig, in Ottawa.

"Kidcasting" in my basement at three, reciting *Alice in Wonderland* from memory. I loved to hear the sound of my own voice played back.

Bylaw Officer Dean. My career lasted only about two weeks in uniform. No dogcatching jokes, please!

My classic rock CHEZ 106 radio days. "Coming up . . . Aerosmith!"

The glamour shot I attached to every single résumé, even after it was off by many years and several pounds.

My going-away party in Ottawa before I left for New York City and the Imus job, with my girlfriends Lianne, Shirley, and Cyndi. If she can make it there . . .

Hosting my own radio program, *The Broad Perspective*, on CFRA Ottawa.

My favorite meet-the-rock-star story of all time: Steven Tyler. It took me twenty years to get him to sign the photo. He delivered.

The day my friends Lianne and Tony met Sean (*middle*) in Hawaii. And the rest of my life began.

Husband and wife. Sean and I getting married at New York City Hall, June 8, 2007.

The *Freddy the Frogcaster* signing with my sweet tadpoles, Matthew and Theodore.

My hero, Neil Cavuto.

There's life before you get kissed by Harry Connick Jr. and then life after. . . .

A welcome-home celebration with my friends Ainsley, Brian, and Steve the day I came back after being away for two months from the neck nightmare.

Trying out a new MS therapy, an infusion I get once a month. So far so good . . .

Dreams do come true! Singing back up for Lynyrd Skynyrd. Turn it up!

to ruin the town's annual picnic and how Freddy was the only one to get the forecast right that day. He and his friends made sure there was shelter to take cover and umbrellas to stay dry. Cheryl found a talented illustrator named Russ Cox who made Freddy leap off the page. The book was fun, with a good lesson on how we can prepare in advance when bad weather arrives to help keep each other safe. I was incredibly proud of it. When the first copies arrived at my doorstep, it was one of the most exciting, satisfying achievements of my career.

Freddy the Frogcaster was set to be released in the summer of 2013. I was so proud of this book, and myself. Then, right before its release, I was told my job was changing. Quite drastically.

For close to a decade I was the nine-to-five daytime meteorologist on Fox News. I filled in on *Fox & Friends* once in a while as well if there was a big story to cover. For many years my friend Steve Doocy did weather on *Fox & Friends*—he was a forecaster back in Kansas at one point—and then it was decided they would hire an additional person Monday through Friday for the morning show. For a few months I split the shift with a beautiful full-time meteorologist named Maria Molina.

Then I found out Maria was going to be doing *Fox & Friends* on weekdays. I would move to covering Monday through Wednesday from noon to prime time (evenings) and then weekends noon to prime time.

I was embarrassed, ashamed, and upset. Why wasn't I considered for the job? I called my husband to tell him.

He was mad. "You've got to work weekends now? When will we get to spend time as a family? This is bullshit." I told him that maybe it was time to look for another job.

I decided that even though my full-time job was changing, I was going to make sure this children's book author side gig was successful.

I asked Lauren Petterson, VP of morning programming, if I could launch the book on their morning show even though I was technically no longer doing the program apart from filling in from time to time on the weekends. Lauren was always a cheerleader of mine and told me they would be honored to do the first interview and promote the heck out of it. I remember being so nervous the day of the book launch because I felt like a failure for not being good enough to be on their show. I felt sick to my stomach in the hair and makeup chair, but I wanted to smile through the moment and sell this new book along with possibly a different career path somewhere down the road.

I decided to wear yellow to help brighten my mood and help convey a sunny message with my friend Freddy. Lauren came up with a great idea to ask coworkers and friends to bring their kids onto the set to help promote the book. It turned out to be a great interview, and *Freddy the Frogcaster* quickly became a bestseller.

The book was a hit and gave me self-confidence when I needed it. Because I was working weekends and had time during the week, I went to schools, libraries, and bookstores to read to kids and talk about what it was like to do the weather and write about it. I loved performing in front of children and the interactions with them were the best part. Kids became so excited when talking about the big storms they had experienced. And they would get so animated when I asked them to do the weather in front of their friends and classmates. I realized I was really good at this. Teachers and principals would tell me they wanted more of this at their schools, and word spread. I was getting more requests to come to speak and read *Freddy.* Sean helped me make a PowerPoint presentation to show kids what happens when I wear green on the green screen and how magically I turn into a floating head on the big weather map. They would laugh when I told them weather forecasting was hard but learning how to do the forecast on the green screen took a lot of practice as well. At the beginning of my forecasting career I had to write the words "East Coast" and "West Coast" on my right and left hands to remind me which direction to point in. I loved hearing their giggles.

I read the book with all the different voices for each character and talked about the lessons we learn and how we can prepare for storms. I figured if I could tap into their excitement about weather, then it would take the scare out of a potentially dangerous storm that could affect them in the future.

One of the biggest compliments I get from parents and teachers who have read my *Freddy the Frogcaster* books is that kids want to get involved and be proactive when it comes to severe weather. Many families have gotten emergency preparedness kits for their homes and cars after reading the stories. Parents say they are happy to have a resource to explain why certain weather events happen, and they feel calmer and more in control when they face an emergency.

Since the first book did so well, I was asked to do four more. Freddy has covered thunderstorms, a big blizzard, a terrible tornado, a huge hurricane, and a flash flood. While I was promoting the flash flood book, Hurricane Harvey was in the process of unleashing an unprecedented 60 inches of rain on southeastern Texas, so I decided to give the proceeds from that book to an organization called Team Rubicon made up of volunteer veterans and retired first responders who go out to disaster zones to help recover and rebuild.

I've spoken to thousands of kids and helped spread the word about weather safety. I've had parents tell me their kids have memorized the Freddy books and can read them from memory (just like I used to do as a kid back home in Canada reading *Alice in Wonderland*). There's even a Freddy app I created for kids to track their local forecast and play dress-up Freddy, depending on what the weather is like each day.

My weather books were one of the reasons I was given the incredible honor of being inducted into the Meteorologist Hall of Fame in Punxsutawney, Pennsylvania, along with some other pretty amazing forecasters and academics. The plaque is proudly displayed in the Punxsutawney Weather Discovery Center.

I brought Sean, Matthew, and Theodore to see their mama being honored in the home of the most famous forecasting groundhog in the world. The movie *Groundhog Day* is one of my all-time favorite movies. I still have the worn-out VHS copy in my collection with the hilarious weatherman played by Bill Murray. Just like Phil Connors, we all woke up at 3:00 a.m. and headed to Gobbler's Knob to see the "seer of seers, sage of sages, prognosticator of prognosticators and weather prophet extraordinary" wake up from his long winter's nap to predict whether there would be six more weeks of winter. Just like in the movie, my family and Fox News field producer Samantha Honig stayed at a local bed-and-breakfast with a kind resident named Shirley who has lived in Punxsutawney her whole life.

None of this would have happened without Freddy. My little frogcaster is now being brought into schools as a teaching tool to help kids with their weather lessons. I'm also excited to say we're working on a Freddy animated series that may bring the lily pad to life off the page and onto kids' TV programs and tablets.

Freddy also helped me connect with a kind editor from HarperCollins a little over a year ago when an email popped up on my screen one day at work:

Dear Ms. Dean,

I'm an editor at HarperCollins (the Newscorp book division) and a fan. You know us from publishing recent and forthcoming books from Bret Baier, Ainsley Earhardt and Martha MacCallum.

I've been following your career as a children's book writer, but was wondering if there was a book for grown-ups hiding in your pen?

Eric Nelson

(insert gigantic grin here)

When I go out and talk to kids at schools, not only do I discuss what it's like to be a TV meteorologist, but I also talk about being an author and what it takes to write books. It took seven years from the idea of a children's book (thank you, Governor Kasich) to getting one published. I never forgot about it, and never gave up. The forecast was always bright for Freddy the frogcaster—and his author, who kept on believing in the idea and herself.

Chapter 16

PARACHUTES

July 6, 2016, I was on vacation with my family in Quebec, Canada. I got a text that included a forwarded article from one of my coworkers that read:

> "GRETCHEN CARLSON OF FOX NEWS FILES
> HARASSMENT SUIT AGAINST ROGER AILES"

My heart started racing. I started to skim the first few paragraphs from the *New York Times*:

> Roger Ailes, the chairman of Fox News, was accused on Wednesday of forcing out a prominent female anchor after she refused his sexual advances and complained to him about persistent harassment in the newsroom, a startling accusation against perhaps the most powerful man in television news.
>
> In a lawsuit, the anchor, Gretchen Carlson, a longtime Fox

employee who left the network last month, portrays Mr. Ailes as a loutish and serial sexual harasser, accusing him of ogling her in his office, calling her "sexy," and describes a boys' club environment at the network.

Her charges—including the accusation that Mr. Ailes explicitly asked Ms. Carlson for a sexual relationship during a meeting in his office—amounted to an almost unprecedented public attack on Mr. Ailes, a towering figure in media and Republican politics who typically enjoys absolute loyalty from his employees.

Late Wednesday, the parent company of Fox News, 21st Century Fox, issued a measured statement, saying it had "full confidence" in Mr. Ailes, but had initiated an internal review of Ms. Carlson's charges. "We take these matters seriously," the company said.

Mr. Ailes, in a separate statement, was far less temperate. "Gretchen Carlson's allegations are false," he wrote. "This is a retaliatory suit for the network's decision not to renew her contract," which he attributed to ratings he called "disappointingly low."

I had to read the headline again. Is this for real?

I texted my friend back: "Holy shit."

I forwarded the text and article to Megyn Kelly.

She hadn't seen the story yet and wrote:

"Holy shit."

Megyn Kelly and I have been close friends for over a decade. We've shared a lot with each other over the years, including our past harassment stories about Roger well before all of this was a news story. Our experiences are similar in that we were both targeted in the first year of our new jobs, and then Roger stopped the inappropriate behavior and we both went on to have good working relationships with him. Please note that does not make it right, but back then it was how we navigated. You've seen the news articles and settlements from not just Fox News but other television stations, newspapers, and radio and film studios. Those are news stories because people recognize names and workplaces. It happens everywhere there is a power dynamic. It happened when I was in retail while in high school. It happened with a coworker in my radio days. It happened while I was at *Imus*. I've heard horror stories about the restaurant and high-tech industries. It's not just men, either. Stories of abusive, powerful women are coming out too.

This behavior has been rampant for decades. We have yet to uncover how pervasive this problem was and probably still is.

As I began reading the whole Gretchen-suing-Ailes article more closely, my family was lined up for the bungee jump machine at Mont Tremblant in Quebec, Canada. Sean shot me a look that said: *Hey, we're on vacation with our children. Put that effing phone away.*

I passed my phone over to show him the news headline. His eyes widened, and he told me to go ahead and do what I needed to do. He would take care of the kids. My husband thankfully knows when he needs to take over the parenting duties, but he is also a good reminder that the phone needs to disappear when we are on a family vacation.

Gretchen and I were friendly when she worked at Fox. I filled in occasionally on *Fox & Friends*, and we had an easygoing rapport on the air. She was funny and would include me in segments. Over the years we certainly shared stories of balancing family and career.

I had shared some of my story about my Roger job interview at the hotel lobby and the bizarre phone sex request at a dinner with Gretchen and a Fox News makeup artist. I also remember her asking about it again several months before she was let go from Fox. She also asked me if I knew of anyone else Roger had crossed a line with.

Over the years I did know of a few other women who had shared fairly tame but disturbing Roger stories with me, but we just chalked them up to the business we were in and Roger being Roger. Most of these stories were like mine. He was suggestive, testing the waters, throwing out the line to see if we would take the bait. Sometimes he would call women up to the office under false pretenses, like talking about their careers, and then he would act inappropriately. He would sometimes begin offering solid career advice and then see how far he could go with the sex talk.

Was it creepy? Yes. Did it make us feel uncomfortable? Yes. Could we do anything about it? Well, if we went to HR, our stories would go right back to Roger. We could always try to get another job, I suppose, but many of us had to support our families. For me, navigating the suggestive Roger remarks or trips to his office was a trade-off, because I loved my job and the people I worked with.

Also, back then my stories were nothing compared to what I now know was happening to other women. In our conversations over the years, Gretchen never told me anything had happened to her. We all heard rumors about other women, but in this business rumors run rampant.

I was and am friends with many of my women coworkers at Fox. As the weather lady, I'm in a unique position of not being a threat to anyone's job. This business can be fiercely competitive, and for females, I think it's hard to trust each other sometimes for fear of being backstabbed or left behind for a better job. Megyn always called me a "soft place to fall" for other women to talk to. "Like a large personal pillow?" I would joke.

Some of the female staff had confided in me with their Roger stories. There was a coworker that came into my office crying one day after a meeting with Mr. Ailes. He had asked her to make a demo reel of some of her hosting and reporting duties. She was excited to go and talk to him, get advice, and maybe stay on his radar if there were any job openings. My friend had mentioned many times to me that she wanted her career to move to the next level. She was ready for new challenges. I wished her good luck on the day of the meeting and gave her a bit of a pep talk. She came in early, made an appointment to get her hair and makeup done beforehand, put on her best dress, and confidently took the elevator to the second floor.

When it was over she came back to my office and began to cry. I asked her what was wrong and gently inquired if Mr. Ailes had done anything to make her upset. But she didn't talk. She just sobbed. I hugged her and said it was okay. She just said she was having a bad day, so I didn't pry any further. But I always assumed he had done or said something that crossed the line.

There wasn't really a place we could safely go and complain. We all knew HR was not a true human resources department (at the time), and all the stories that were brought to their attention were funneled down to one person: Roger. Roger was the king. He saw and heard everything.

Megyn called me about an hour after our "Holy shit" texts and we started to discuss the unbelievable developments. I had to duck out of a water park in Quebec to go into the women's bathroom to talk in hushed tones to my friend about a sexual harassment lawsuit against the most powerful man in cable news

Neither of us thought Gretchen had a chance against Roger. Still, Megyn and I started to think about all the women that this COULD have happened to.

I was still in Canada for the week, but Megyn and I were talking or texting several times a day. There were many calls at midnight after her show, *The Kelly File*, until the early hours of the morning. She was telling me what it was like around the office. There were Team Roger ringleaders going around to female anchors to get them on the record verbally or in writing that they were on the side of Roger against Gretchen. It was implied that if they didn't pledge allegiance, there would be repercussions.

During this time I started to hear bits and pieces of more stories from my women coworkers, both past and present. I was not the only one who had witnessed bad behavior from the boss. Although I believe some anchors had never been harassed by Roger, I believe there were more of us who were called into Roger's office and had uncomfortable situations with him at some point in our careers.

Then the articles started to come out from those who supported Roger. A "Gretchen is lying" camp had been set up. Word had gotten to Megyn that she was expected to issue a statement in support of Roger, since she was the biggest female anchor at Fox. Because she was also a victim of his harassment, she couldn't in good conscience go on the record and defend him. By the way, Megyn has said this and documented it, but she did go to a supervisor and complain about Roger's advances in the early days of her career at Fox News. This supervisor had told her, "Just try and avoid him."

No matter how powerful he was or how badly we needed our jobs, we wouldn't say Roger wasn't capable of harassment. Megyn wouldn't do it. I wouldn't do it. There were now many articles and newspaper stories quoting other anchors who claimed they could never believe Roger could have this dark side. Loud? Obnoxious? Inappropriate? Sure. But sexually harass women? That was not the Roger they knew.

The media noticed that Megyn Kelly wasn't saying anything in support of Roger. Meanwhile, the amount of Fox News talent that was publicly going to bat for the boss made Megyn's silence deafening. She felt the slings and arrows being aimed at her from people she worked with and in the barrage of social media attacks.

Megyn was hearing from people on Team Roger who were furious that she was not issuing a statement showing her support for the man who had helped make her a star.

Meanwhile, Arthur Aidala, who was a criminal defense lawyer and at one time a Fox News contributor, was being asked for legal advice to help Roger. He called many on-air talent and asked them to speak on behalf of Mr. Ailes. That included Megyn. It was reportedly at the request of Roger's wife, Beth Ailes, that Arthur kept asking Megyn to lend her voice and support. She refused. Then Mrs. Ailes called Megyn personally.

Megyn told Beth that she had been advised to not speak publicly during the investigation and that she hoped Mrs. Ailes would understand.

Then something critical happened. One night Megyn called me and told me that she had heard the "investigation" into Gretchen's allegations was a sham. An insider called it a whitewash: it only included a very small group of interviews. In other words, Roger wasn't going anywhere. It was just for show.

We were furious. Megyn decided she needed to make a call to someone higher up.

At the time, Lachlan Murdoch was the executive chairman of 21st Century Fox. Despite having only spoken with Lachlan once prior to this, she decided to reach out as an obligation to tell him this investigation needed to be legitimate and that there was reason to believe Ailes might have been harassing women.

Megyn decided to share her own story about Roger, and she explained that she wasn't the only one who had had that experience. Within three days of that call, on July 11, 2016, it was announced that 21st Century Fox had hired an outside law firm, Paul, Weiss, Rifkind, Wharton, and Garrison, to conduct a full and fair investigation into Roger. Megyn Kelly was immediately called in.

Megyn was planning to tell Paul Weiss all the details of the harassment she had experienced during her first year at Fox News. She also asked my permission to tell my story, since I never got a request to cooperate in the investigation.

After her Paul Weiss meeting, she called and said it had gone well. Megyn recounted her days as a young reporter getting calls from Roger, the meetings in his office, the inappropriate comments and suggestions, and the attempted physical contact. When the lawyers asked her if she knew any other women that had experienced this, she told them my name and what I had told her.

I was to expect a phone call from Paul Weiss soon to ask me to come in the next day.

Throughout all of this, I was telling Sean everything. Every night we were going over the latest details. I was forwarding him articles to keep in a file. We knew that I could easily lose my job going against Roger. None of us believed he would be fired. At times I felt embarrassed and ashamed, especially after the crap I had to endure with Imus. Sean was steadfast and said he was behind me 100 percent. I had to tell the truth. It was more important than the job.

I was trying to hold it together through these incredibly stressful few weeks. I wasn't sleeping; we were all trying to do our jobs while this earthquake was happening within our company. There were whispers and looks along with gossip and many closed-door meetings.

My breaking point came the night before I went to tell Paul Weiss my story. I was starting to get cold feet. Was telling my story about what had happened over a decade ago worth risking my job? I was the primary breadwinner. Without my salary, we could not afford our mortgage or our current way of life. My kids were happy and healthy. We had a fantastic school, a safe neighborhood, someone to help with our kids, and a decent health care plan that helped us with the expensive MS drugs I was taking.

I was riding home in the late afternoon on the Long Island Rail Road (LIRR) from work and began to freak out about going against Roger. I texted Megyn and said, "I don't know if we should do this. Our families depend on us. Is it worth risking our jobs and careers to go against the most powerful man in cable news?"

Megyn wrote me back and asked where I was. Could she call me? "Don't back down now!"

I told her I was on the LIRR and I couldn't talk but that I would call her when I got home.

When I arrived, Sean could tell by my demeanor that I wasn't myself. I began confessing that I thought maybe this was not the right thing to do. "I don't know if I can risk my job and what we've built by going in and telling my story. Roger will never be let go. If he finds out, we're done. We'll have to move back to Canada. Maybe I should stay out of this."

Sean looked at me. Normally he's very mild-mannered and speaks calmly and thoughtfully, with delicate matters. But he sternly warned:

"You cannot back down now. Do not blink. Finish this. Go in and tell them your story. Tell the truth. Nothing else matters. We'll figure it out."

Then he added:

"By the way, Mama, YOU NEVER THINK CLEARLY WHEN YOU RIDE THE LIRR. THE LIRR IS DEPRESSING. DON'T EVER MAKE BIG DECISIONS ON THE LIRR. NOTHING GOOD EVER COMES ON THE LIRR."

I laughed nervously and called Megyn. I told her I had had a momentary lapse of reason on the LIRR, and I told her what Sean had said about riding and making decisions on that hour-long train ride from the office to Long Island. She laughed her wonderful laugh and said:

"I will pay for a car service when you go into Paul Weiss. Do not ride the LIRR when you go for that meeting."

The moral of the story here is: Never make life-changing decisions when you're on public transit.

Sean was also the one who suggested I write everything down before I went for my meeting with Paul Weiss, from my recollection of what had happened with Roger before and after I was hired to a list of names of women I had talked to or suspected had had similar experiences.

On top of all of this, I had to give myself my MS shot. (We did injections three times a week.) All this stress pointed to a flare-up waiting to happen.

Sean gave me the shot and brought me a glass of wine. I was going over everything in my mind about what I would say at the lawyer's office. I took one sip of wine, and that's when I ran to the bathroom and threw up. I started shaking, and my whole body broke out in hives. My eyes swelled up, and I was crying uncontrollably. I couldn't stop sobbing, shaking, and then hyperventilating. This was all too much. Roger was never going to get fired, and I knew he would find out I had gone against him. What was I doing? I curled up in a ball on the floor. The door was closed. I didn't want my kids to hear me. Sean came in and was visibly worried. This had never happened before: I couldn't talk. He carried me into our bedroom and got me under the blankets. I was freezing and shaking. I couldn't calm down.

It took about an hour for me to finally stop trembling. I talked to Megyn, and she told me we were doing the right thing. The truth would set us free. If Roger was not a serial harasser, he had nothing to fear. And if he was, all the more reason to speak up. She again insisted I take a car service to the Paul Weiss appointment and warned: DO NOT RIDE THE LIRR. She got me to laugh.

I asked both an allergist and my therapist, Judy, about what had happened the night before I went in to the lawyers. Was it an allergy? Was it the MS drug reacting badly? They told me there is no question that I had had a panic attack. This was the first panic attack I had ever had in my life. It was one of the scariest things I've ever gone through.

July 18, 2016, I took a car service into midtown Manhattan and walked into the office of Paul Weiss and told them what I had experienced with Roger Ailes and how uncomfortable it was seeing my coworkers coming out and saying we were liars and that this was not the boss they knew and loved. I told them about some of the women I had talked to who had their own stories. I also mentioned that everything was controlled by Roger. Everything went through Roger. We were all petrified of him finding out that we were going against him.

When the lawyers asked if I had told anyone else my Roger stories while they were occurring, I admitted the only person at the time whom I had told was my therapist. They asked if they could get written consent from Judy. I told them I would give it to them.

A day or so later, Megyn told me that she was hearing that even though she and I had told our stories, and a few other women had come forward, too few women had volunteered to speak. There was so much pressure on them by prominent Fox personalities backing Roger.

Then I did something very risky. I reached out to my female coworkers who I knew had a Roger story and asked if I could come to see them in their offices to talk. One by one I told them my experiences with the boss, how even though I was risking my career I told the lawyers at Paul Weiss my uncomfortable experiences with

Mr. Ailes. If we all went in and shared our stories, it could make a difference in the future for women at this company and elsewhere. We could all make a change somehow. I talked to them in person and on the phone. I listened to their stories and cried with them, reminding them that there is strength in numbers and we were all in this together.

Some didn't want to speak out for fear of retaliation, but some of them at great risk and peril to their careers and livelihoods risked everything and did tell their stories.

My husband, Sean, was increasingly worried about my under-ground networking. Every time I reached out to someone else, the odds were even greater that our plan would be uncovered. He mentioned this several times. It was one thing for me to tell my story; it was quite another to play this dangerous game, trying to find other women to talk. It would just take one woman to go to Team Roger, and our little secret army would be exposed.

Our stories never got out. But Megyn's did. In a July 19 article by *New York* magazine's Gabriel Sherman, the headline read:

"SOURCES: MEGYN KELLY TOLD MURDOCH INVESTIGATORS THAT ROGER AILES SEXUALLY HARASSED HER"

Megyn was furious that someone had leaked her story, but the upside to this was that more women came forward. In the days to come, we would start to hear more stories about Roger's pervasive behavior.

The slow *drip drip drip* of stories that were surfacing included some about former employees who had very dark stories about Roger Ailes. Back when I first started at Fox, I had heard rumors of one former employee who might have been having an affair with Roger. He apparently took "extra care of her" for many years. After the Gretchen lawsuit news broke, there was a bombshell report about how he had tortured her mentally and physically for two decades. I read that he asked to have phone sex with her—and then I remembered he did the same with me when he called me at home before I was hired. Her hotel liaisons with Mr. Ailes were at the same place he asked to meet me for a drink years ago—the Renaissance Times Square Hotel. It all rang true. And made me sick to my stomach.

On July 21, 2016, Roger Ailes resigned just a few months shy of the twentieth anniversary of the network he founded. He denied all the allegations that were brought against him up until the day he died a year later.

On September 6, Gretchen Carlson was awarded $20 million as a settlement from 21st Century Fox with an unprecedented apology. And later, several other Fox News former and current employees were given settlements and signed NDAs.

Some of my silent army don't work at Fox anymore. Some of us do. I never asked for or received a payment or signed an NDA.

So this is my story. Many things have happened in the broadcasting industry since the shakeup at Fox News. Many women became brave. A little silent underground army of Fox women—all of whom were actively employed by Fox and had much to lose—did this . . . long before there was a #metoo hashtag.

I'm proud of all of us. Together, our stories helped stop some pervasive, humiliating, horrible behavior from a powerful boss, and it was a turning point to more women feeling their power to speak their truths about sexual harassment in the workplace. Many risked their jobs, their families' primary incomes, their personal safety, and their careers.

Megyn wrote it perfectly in her chapter "Pay It Forward" in her bestselling book *Settle for More:*

The passive role felt more obligatory; an active one raised the stakes considerably.

But could I stay silent? What if there were other victims? What if—God forbid—he was still doing it to someone? The choice became clear: honor my ethical code or abide by my loyalty to Roger. I couldn't do both.

I expect to get questions of "Why didn't you report the behavior? Why didn't you report stories from your coworkers?" Megyn Kelly has the perfect response to that:

You don't get to ask me that question anymore until you ask me first whether there was a safe avenue for reporting in my company. And only if the answer to that is yes do you get to ask question number two.

Very recently, I confessed to a friend that I was going to write about my experience with Roger in my book. She looked at me wide-eyed and asked what had happened. I told her, and she responded with "Well, you've got such a bubbly, fun personality—do you think maybe he mistook that for being flirty?"

I didn't quite know what to say. For an instant, I actually questioned if my personality invited this kind of behavior. And then I had to walk away.

Meanwhile, during this crazy harassment lawsuit tornado, I miraculously had some good news happening in my career.

There was an opening in the weather department on *Fox & Friends*. Maria Molina had gotten married and decided to go back to school to get her doctorate in meteorology in Michigan.

There was a big shift in management post–Fox harassment scandal. Longtime executive Suzanne Scott was promoted to president in charge of programming.

There would be another opportunity to ask to be considered for the *Fox & Friends* role. I asked my husband what he thought.

"Do you want it?"

I told him I did.

He said: "Then go do it. You're a fantastic TV personality, Mama. You shine whenever the camera is on you."

"Even in my midforties?"

"You look better than ever. You tell them you want to be considered."

I made an appointment to see the VP of morning programming, Lauren Petterson, whom I adore. She is a manager, but she has been my cheerleader for many years. She knew how much I wanted to be on *Fox & Friends* over the years and always would send me notes encouraging and supporting me. I sat down with her one morning and told her I had heard Maria was leaving. I told her I wanted to be considered for the position if they were looking for a replacement. She smiled and said, "I would love for you to be on our show. I'm glad you came to me. Let me go in and tell Suzanne Scott you're interested, and so are we!"

I heard a few days later that I was going to get the job.

On November 14, 2016, I got my dream job. Storm clouds made way for sunshine and then a rainbow.

On the day Roger died, we found out during the news during *Fox & Friends*. We were all shocked. I believe that many never knew Roger's evil side, and to this day will defend him despite the overwhelming evidence against him, including what I've just shared. I'd be lying if I told you I didn't still have mixed opinions of him. He could be so good to people: he was so generous with me and kind during my MS diagnosis. Megyn and I still talk about some of the kind and wonderful things Roger did for us back in the day. He should go down as one of the most brilliant men in broadcasting.

For a few minutes, we all remembered the good side of him. We felt for his wife and his son, whom he loved very, very much. There's a video of me crying on the couch out there, saying he would be missed. That was true. But part of me was also crying for those he had abused because of his power. I was weeping for them as well. And as my husband mentioned to me recently, I'm simply just someone who cries. That's just my nature.

In all the interviews I've seen or read about Gretchen, she speaks frequently about her courage and says she "jumped off a cliff" by herself the day she decided to go after Roger Ailes. But let the record show that she had several parachutes with her that day to help break her fall. We didn't have power or money, but we had everything to lose.

And in some ways had more danger to face.

Someday maybe our little underground army will get to tell our stories. For now, I'm glad I had the chance to tell mine.

As for Fox News, the company has made some significant changes when it comes to management and the way human resources is structured. There's even a 1–800 number now for people who would like to submit a complaint anonymously. That was one of the suggestions Megyn and I gave to Paul Weiss to pass along to 21st Century Fox. I'm optimistic for the future of our employees. I've always told new employees that my door is always open if they ever need a friend to talk to or to get advice.

By the way, finally doing my dream job on *Fox & Friends* has been everything I thought it would be and more. Would I be considered for the job if Roger had been in charge? My guess is no. Instead, I heard that Suzanne Scott didn't even blink when Lauren proposed me as their weekday meteorologist. She was excited to tell me about my promotion and has been incredibly supportive—someone who has always kept her door open to me before, during, and after the harassment scandal.

And take note, broadcasting companies that are trying to restructure after harassment and abuse of power lawsuits: Suzanne Scott is as of this writing the ONLY female CEO in all of cable and broadcast news. If you want change, you need to hire more qualified women in positions of power. It's not the only solution, but it will help make a difference. Take it from me. We have so many kickass women here at Fox News who are helping rebuild the management structure from the ground up. My husband, Sean, reminds me of how I've changed since we first met. He says throughout my career I've had so many unsettled moments where I come home angry and/or upset. That doesn't happen anymore. After twenty-five years, I can honestly say I feel at peace in my work environment. It's not perfect, but I no longer believe my voice won't be heard, or that I'll be told to just steer clear of a person or problem.

At the age of forty-eight, I'm doing a job I absolutely love. It doesn't feel like work—it's being part of a family. I believe every single one of the jobs I've done along the way has led up to this. At this point in my career, I feel like there's nothing else I'd rather be doing. The moral of this story is: Never give up. Keep challenging yourself. Step up when you need to and ask for what you think you deserve. Someone will always be your cheerleader. I feel very lucky I've had great friends and mentors in my life who have cared and listened, offering advice, guidance, and support. Especially when the storm clouds were closing in. And when it's time to hang up the microphone, I will do it with such pride. I know I made a difference, and in my own way maybe helped a young woman starting out in this business to not be afraid anymore.

I read a quote the other day from one of my favorite funny female voices, Erma Bombeck, that brought a smile to my face. It's a nice way to end this chapter in this book and in my life.

She wrote:

"When I stand before God at the end of my life, I would hope that I would not have a single bit of talent left, and I could say, 'I used everything you gave me.'"

Amen, Erma.

Amen.

Chapter 17

UNPACKING BOXES WITH JUDY

It wasn't until I moved to New York and found myself in a constant state of misery that I decided I needed help. The Imus job was the breaking point. I would cry daily after work. It was hard to sleep. I felt anxious all the time. I was questioning all my choices in life. There was a feeling of hopelessness almost like a bottomless pit. Was my career that important to me? It certainly wasn't giving me the gratification that I always thought it would. Being in New York at what should've been the job of a lifetime was a complete letdown. What exactly was I searching for?

For many years I was pushing aside feelings and events in my life that were difficult to revisit. I was an excellent compartmentalizer. My relationship with my dad became nonexistent, so I just tried to keep it in a box and not open it up very often. My relationship with my mom was fractured as well, especially after my father left. It was easy to blame her, because she was the one my brother, Craig, and I still had contact with. I had difficulty talking to her about these feelings I was having, and I was resentful. Because our dad wasn't around very much growing up, she was our primary parent, and we fought a lot. I was stubborn and always wanted my way. She had given up a good career to be a stay-at-home mom. I sensed she wasn't always happy with her choice to be at home with us, and I felt her unhappiness with my dad. We moved around a lot in just a few years, and there were fights about money, his workaholism, and his reclusiveness. I remember one of my essays for English class in middle school started off with: "A beautiful house that we lived in for such a short time now has a for sale sign in the front yard. My childhood is packed away in boxes in the hallways where I used to run and play."

When it comes to therapy, I relate the work on ourselves to unpacking boxes of memories that have been sealed up and stored up in the attic of our brain.

My therapist, Judy, was the one who picked me up and began to piece me back together when I finally began falling apart. Together we started unpacking years of boxes that were sealed away in the far corners of my mind.

And although it is her job to help people, I consider her a person who has made one of the biggest impacts on my life. She knows me better than most, in some ways even better than my mom, my closest friends, or Sean. She has helped me through my deepest, darkest moments. There were times during some of our sessions when she would sit and listen for fifty minutes and then say, "You deserve to be angry and upset. What human being wouldn't be?"

The only other time I had ever gotten help from a therapist was when I went through the home invasion in Houston, and that was just for a short time. Realistically, I should've kept going to see the woman I was assigned to through our health insurance plan, but I remember not liking her very much. She acted like a know-it-all when

I was going through the shock of the event with different stages of anger, grief, and depression. I never went back after the week I saw her, so I never fully processed what had happened. Friends and family seemed to treat me a little differently too. Word spreads quickly when you're a victim of a crime or assault. People mean well, but it's gossip nonetheless. I remember confiding in a childhood friend after it happened and she then shared the story with members of her family. When I attended her wedding, I could tell from their weird looks and bizarre questions they all knew. "Ahh, yes, the friend from Houston . . ."

When I moved to New York and was going through the Imus days, that was when things began to spiral out of control. I was in a constant state of feeling overwhelmed, beaten down, and insecure. I asked my friend Lou who worked with me if he knew of anyone. (He of all people knew that I needed someone to talk to and help getting through some of those tough, abusive days.) He had a buddy whose mom knew of a therapist whose office was close by. Her name was Judy. I thought of the classic song "Suite: Judy Blue Eyes" by Crosby, Stills & Nash, which I had played probably hundreds of times.

The classic rock DJ in me must tell you the significance of that song. It was written for Judy Collins, who was Stephen Stills's former girlfriend, about their imminent breakup. Judy Collins was also a famous singer and songwriter known for her piercing blue eyes.

The first thing I noticed about Judy when I sat down in her office was her kind blue eyes: The windows of the soul.

Judy has helped me through some tremendously challenging periods. The daily stress from Imus was a big topic of discussion for us. For many months I felt like this was normal behavior and I was the one that had issues.

Was there something about my personality that made him lash out and constantly belittle me, call me fat, stupid, and useless? Once in a blue moon he would praise me and tell me I was doing a good job. I would feel I was turning a corner, like *He likes me, he really does like me!* And then it would be right back to the yelling, then ignoring and pretending I didn't exist or picking on what I looked like or how terrible I was. Judy told me right off the bat this wasn't normal behavior. It was abusive, and we had to find a way to get away from it. No one deserved to be treated that way.

When I met Sean, I kept telling her the last thing I needed was a relationship or a boyfriend in my life. She told me that not every man needed to be a boyfriend. Why couldn't we just enjoy each other's company and be accepting of a new friend? Someone who was kind and helpful? Didn't I deserve people like that in my life?

Judy also helped me process my relationship with my father. When I tracked him down and we started emailing back and forth, I would print out our poisonous exchanges for her to look at. Was this appropriate behavior between a father and a daughter? Why did he disappear and not want to be in touch with his children?

She told me none of this was my fault. My father had big issues of his own that had probably never been addressed or dealt with. And more than likely he had mental problems and depression from events that went back into his childhood. Sadly, the story of fathers leaving and not keeping in touch with their kids is a lot more common than you'd think.

We also talked about the home invasion and the assault. I had tried to deny the shock and guilt I felt over being robbed and not fighting back somehow. Sean tells me when I told him about this terrible night that he could tell it had deeply affected me and was still raw and unprocessed. Judy helped me get through those feelings and thoughts that had never been fully dealt with.

And then the Roger Ailes harassment. When the lawyers from Paul Weiss asked in July of 2016 if I had told anyone about Roger and his inappropriate behavior, I admitted that Sean knew a little but that I had disclosed all of it with Judy while it was happening. They asked my permission to talk to her, and I had to give written consent for them to contact her. I did feel incredibly vulnerable sharing the fact that I used a therapist on a regular basis to these strangers. I felt in a way it showed weakness.

After Judy talked to the lawyers, she told me she made sure to add:

"For the record, Janice is an incredibly strong, well-adjusted woman. I can vouch for her integrity and character." That brought tears to my eyes.

And then, of course, my MS diagnosis. On the outside, I tried to be strong throughout the weeks, months, and years after I was told I had MS, but there were so many days of fear, anxiety, depression, and the unknown. She was there through it all. She even educated herself on the disease when I told her I had it so she could understand it and help me as best she could. She introduced meditation and breathing exercises I could do when I could feel my heart starting to race.

Having children, I was always struggling with whether I could be a good mother. For a person who was driven by career and success for most of her life, how would it be possible to slow down and put my focus and attention on a baby? Judy would tell me over and over about what a great mom I would be. She also made me realize how miraculous our bodies are, to try to help me stop thinking about the flaws and embrace the fact that a life was created and growing in this amazing body of mine.

Judy also pointed out having children could help repair the relationship with my mom.

She always used to tell me: "When you have kids, you may look at your mother differently. You may begin to understand her more." She was right. My boys adore their grandma Stella.

When I see Matthew and Theodore with Mom, I can picture how she was with my brother and me growing up. When I listen to her read to them, I close my eyes and pretend I am their age. She has such an animated way about her when she is with them, and can make them giggle with a quick joke or a look. Over the years she has come on *Fox & Friends* for birthdays and celebrations, and she takes over the room with her stories and wit. She confessed to me one time that when she posted a video of one of her appearances on television, her girlfriends all told her she missed her calling.

I was recently sick from the flu while my mom was in New York visiting us. I couldn't get out of bed, so she took over and helped with the kids. I had a fever, so Mom was coming into my bedroom with ginger ale and changing a cold washcloth on my head every few minutes to bring my fever down. Just like she used to do when I was little. It made me realize you're never too old to have your mother take care of you.

I now know that my mom was always there for me. Even when we were far apart. It took many years of hard work and therapy to remove the old bandages and let the wounds heal.

Judy provided a safe harbor when the seas were too rough. A calm, peaceful place where there was no judgment. Someone to listen, pass tissues, offer a suggestion, or just be there. A place to breathe after unpacking some of those boxes.

I show her pictures of my kids, and she will look at them and smile. "How handsome they are, Janice. Look at this beautiful family you have. Be proud of this life and yourself."

I often tell her we did some very important work together. I would not be the person I am today without Judy.

I talk very openly to my friends and family about the fact that I see a therapist. And although it is a little more accepted in society to seek help, there's still a certain stigma attached to paying someone to talk about ourselves. I now believe getting into therapy shows incredible strength and self-awareness.

There are still so many myths when it comes to seeing a therapist— like you must be seriously disturbed. And while there are those who specialize in severe emotional issues, many therapists focus on every-day challenges like career changes, parenting, stress management, or navigating life changes, like a divorce or death in the family.

A therapist can simply help be a problem solver. I know that Judy won't criticize, or interrupt. And my conversations with her are confidential, so I feel free to say something without worrying about someone's feelings or damaging a relationship.

Many people think visiting a therapist means digging up skeletons from your childhood. And while Judy and I certainly talked about my issues growing up, we spent more time talking about the present-day reality and the future I wanted to create for myself.

I've always encouraged people to talk to someone if they're confused or going through a difficult time. You have very little to lose and potentially a lot to gain in clarity, self-awareness, and happiness.

There are those who decide to use medication to manage their feelings and anxiety. While I think this can help in the short term, over the long term, if you don't work on yourself and what you're going through, the problems might never go away.

Health insurance in many cases will help pay for therapy. It's worthwhile to investigate this in any health care plan. I know many people who pay a lot of money for their gym memberships and personal trainers. For me, Judy was a personal trainer for my brain to strengthen my mental muscles.

Whenever I find myself getting anxious about schedules or a busy calendar or all the things we have to do on a weekly basis, she says, "Don't go there till you get there!" Meaning: Stay in the present and don't worry too much about the future, which we sometimes have no control over.

It's hard to believe I've been seeing Judy for fifteen years of my life. When I visit her, I have to smile, because the waiting room hasn't changed and neither has her office. I imagine myself as that insecure, frantic thirty-two-year-old woman sitting in front of this kind motherly lady with the pretty blue eyes, short, curly hair, and sensible shoes.

Nowadays our visits are much more infrequent. I remember the day when she told me, "Janice, we don't need to see each other every week. It's up to you, but I think the work we have done together has been very successful. Look at you now. Look how far you've come. I'll always be here, but I believe you no longer need my help."

I couldn't bear not to have Judy in my life, so we do catch-up sessions every four to six months now, and she's always a phone call away if I need her. I did see her regularly when the Paul Weiss investigation was underway, but I'm back to checking in with her every six months or so. I told her I was writing this book, and she wasn't surprised. She told me that we used to talk about me writing a book about my life someday. She said she couldn't wait to read it, that I would help a lot of people. I am a big believer in therapy. Judy was my shelter during many storms.

Many days I would think I had nothing to tell her. My week had gone pretty well without any crisis or need to talk things through. Then I would be a little shocked when she said "Our time is up" and I realized we had filled up our time together. Somehow we still get to squeeze a few more minutes in about the books we are reading.

At the end of every visit, she would let me hug her. I'm not sure when we began our hugs, but I remember being in New York, and not knowing a soul, and yearning for a hug. Human contact.

Sometimes I feel like that's all I needed from our visit. Just an embrace from a kind, loving, thoughtful, gentle soul.

Sweet Judy provided the help I needed unpacking all those boxes that cluttered up my head for so many years. And then to help open up the windows to let the fresh air move through. To clear up the cobwebs of old memories and let new ones take their place.

Chapter 18

FACETUNE

Being on TV requires a lot of maintenance. Our visual upkeep is a job in and of itself. The blowouts, the hairspray, the hair extensions, the makeup, the Botox and filler, the false eyelashes, the manicures, the clothing, the jewelry . . . and that's just Geraldo. HA! Just kidding. Geraldo is a rock star and a good friend. And he looks amazing in just a towel. (Check out his Twitter feed, people!)

You get my drift. When I'm not on TV, my hair is up in a clip, and I don't wear makeup at all. My husband, God bless him, says the natural look is when he thinks I look my best.

I've heard about some pretty crazy techniques in this business to stay looking young and thin. From wrapping oneself up in Saran Wrap at night to crazy cleanses and diets.

I am in awe of the discipline some of my fellow anchors have, especially during food segments on *Fox & Friends*. Fortunately for me, I have no desire to be a size 0, and I thoroughly enjoy taste testing every National Pancake Day—or national donut, chocolate chip cookie, or ice cream day. However, I will admit to some cosmetic tweaks here and there. I color and highlight my hair, use the spray tan junk to hide my pasty white skin, squeeze into Spanx every day, and am grateful for our hair and makeup magicians at Fox.

In addition to all of this, technology is also adding to the pressure of looking younger and appearing flawless.

At this stage of my life, I can truthfully say I am the most confident I have ever felt about myself. I remember that when I first started in TV, I would tape every report and replay it for myself, focusing on what I looked like, how I could improve my appearance. I would obsess about my weight, my flaws, things I wished I could fix. But life is a journey, not a destination, and sometimes you forget about the lessons you learn along the way and the signs that tried to warn you of possible danger ahead. Sometimes you take that shortcut to try to get there faster, but it's not always the best route. The universe has a way of reminding us of that.

In this age of selfies and constant social media, we can manipulate our photo image in every way, from hiding imperfections to shrinking our dress sizes. You can whiten your teeth, wipe away wrinkles and blemishes, and even add makeup. All you have to do is download a beauty app on your phone. You can also get a program that automatically airbrushes your flaws as soon as the camera flash goes off on your phone, which I find freaky.

I sometimes shake my head when I see selfies and pictures in which people have overdosed on the facetuning. Some touch themselves up so much they look like a newborn alien. I still want to look like me but perhaps more refreshed, like I've just had eight hours of sleep instead of four or five.

I'm always encouraged when I see more seasoned (not sure if this is a better adjective for "older" . . . it sounds like we're baking a chicken) or how about "mature," women who are embracing their age and still rocking it.

Helen Mirren is a good example of this. I think she's more beautiful now than when she was in her twenties and thirties.

Having been at Fox for over fifteen years, I am blessed with hair and makeup stylists who perform small miracles on us. Before Fox, I was my own stylist, and you may recall my Imus coworkers referencing the similarities between myself and Robin Williams when he was dressed up in *Mrs. Doubtfire*. I didn't have the time or the patience to smooth my hair or add eyelashes or lip gloss.

Over the years I've also come to appreciate the magic of good studio lighting. Our new *Fox & Friends* studio takes years off of our faces. And there's also a portable light they will shine in our visages that blasts out the wrinkles and makes us look all "glowy." I've joked with Anthony and Chris, our lighting technicians ("lighting genius" is what it should say on their résumés), that if I ever win the lottery, I will pay them tons of money to be my personal lighting assistants so wherever I go they can just power up this big, beautiful light and shine it below my face. And what the hell: if I'm that rich, I'm also going to have someone that carries around a fan so I can look like I'm in a Beyoncé music video. I'm kidding! (Sort of.)

These days you can walk into a dermatologist's office and in just minutes have those lines around your face filled up with injectables. That little serum called Botox—made from the bacteria that causes botulism—has changed the cosmetic industry. Yes, it's the same botulism that in high doses causes food poisoning. In tiny amounts, this little poison potion can temporarily smooth out frown lines or wrinkles as it blocks nerve activity in the muscles. The injected muscle can't contract, so the wrinkles can relax and soften. There are sometimes mistakes in the world of Botox in which you can have an eyelid droop or a lopsided facial feature or smile: a facial droop. In this business, they call it "Bad Botox." I've known a few anchors this has happened to, and they have to take time off work until it wears off.

I have used Botox for a few years now. I tried it right after my youngest son, Theodore, was born, to take out the creases between my eyebrows. And then I graduated to the forehead. I still want to have some expression in my face, so I don't do as much, and I wait a little longer to get it done again. I'm scared to try fillers because I see some TV and movie personalities who have "filled up" too much and have that bizarre puffy, shiny cheek thing happening. My dermatologist tells me that if you use fillers the proper way, you won't have that happen. I'll let you know when I try it out. I don't mind injectables as long as they're done properly and safely. Hey, if it makes you feel better about yourself, I'm all for it. That goes for any cosmetic surgery. My feeling is if you've educated yourself on the possible risks and/or side effects, and your husband or wife or family are okay with it, then go for it. I learned the hard way that sometimes these new lasers, potions, and magic wands can do damage.

A few years ago I asked a doctor if there was anything he could do with my neck. I've had a bad relationship with my neck since I was little. There are weird lines around it like a tree trunk. They've been there since I was a baby. Now in my late forties, I noticed some excess skin gathering around like an accordion in the middle. Like the tree rings, you could probably guess my age just by counting the lines around my neck. If I could wear turtlenecks and scarves for the rest of my life, I would. I've had many conversations with women my age about our aging necks. And as much as we want to believe those late-night infomercials on the latest creams to firm and tighten our loose skin, it's a little too good to be true.

Someone told me she worked with an anchor who would pinch the loose skin at the back of her neck and use duct tape to hold it back for the three hours that she was on the air while keeping her hair long to hide the tape. I have not tried this, but I can certainly identify. And who knew duct tape would provide such a potential quick fix to turkey neck? One of my girlfriends who's in the business told me a story in which two sisters came up to her at an event and wanted to get a picture. She said no problem, and the sisters then asked her for a favor before they snapped the shot.

"Okay . . . ," she said a little suspiciously.

They asked if she could be in the middle—one sister on each side—while they instructed my friend to put her hands on the backs of their necks and hold their loose skin tightly so it looked smooth for them in the picture. I kid you not. I may ask my friend to do the same for me the next time we're together and get our picture taken.

Holy moly. I'm glad I'm not alone.

So, after my constant questions every visit to the doctor's office about my literal turtleneck, he told me there was a procedure called "Fractora" he was starting to use. It was an outpatient procedure done in the office; it takes under an hour and regenerates your natural collagen and tightens that old skin. My eyes widened, and I felt my endorphins dancing a happy dance.

Clasping my hands lightly with a lilt in my voice like a little girl, I asked how long this miracle treatment would last (forgetting the old expression "If it sounds too good to be true, it probably is"). He said it could tighten my neck for several years.

YESSSSSSS!

I asked about the downtime.

He said, "About five days . . ." I quickly looked at my calendar to see when my kids were on spring break; that way I could be off with them as my new tight neck healed itself. I was already imagining myself in pretty V-neck dresses without feeling I should be gobbling all the way to Thanksgiving dinner.

I went home and told my husband I wanted to do this. Sean hates the idea of any kind of surgery or injecting anything into my face, but he knows this crazy visual business I'm in that requires occasional "tune-ups." I've promised him I would never have surgery to pull things back or upward. And that goes for boob jobs. As long as there's Spanx and push-up bras, I'm okay with letting it all hang out after my last weather report. But the neck thing drives me nuts.

"Okay, okay," Sean said. "I know you've hated your neck since I started dating you."

Hmmm . . . Was I that obvious?

I penciled in the date on the calendar: the Friday before spring break. I took out my credit card. It wasn't cheap—a couple of mortgage payments (eek)—but I was already dreaming about my dormant collagen coming back to life.

I told a few people—my close friends at work and some girlfriends—but I kept it kind of quiet because I figured no one would find out. It was February and still cold enough outside that when I got back to work, I'd wear some scarves and turtlenecks until my beautiful new smooth neck was ready for its close-up.

I got to my appointment early that morning and cracked a few jokes with the nurses after they gave me two Tylenol:

"Don't you have anything a little harder than this?"

Cue the nervous laughter. They indeed did; they were putting me under for the procedure. I knew this in advance, but I guess I should've figured out that if I'm being given anesthesia, then perhaps it's a little more invasive than just your typical lunchtime fixer-upper. Still, I trusted my doctor. After all, he had a beautiful office in Manhattan.

I was excited to get this done. I thought it would work and with minimal downtime.

An hour later, after I woke up still feeling groggy, the nurses walked me down to where my husband was waiting to drive me home. I remember him looking a little concerned; he didn't say so at the time but later admitted I looked terrible, especially the left side of my face. When I got home, the kids looked a little scared too.

"What happened, Mama? Why do you look like a Q-tip? Are you okay?"

I told them all would be okay. I just had to go to the doctor for a little thing with my neck. This big head and neck bandage would be off tomorrow and I'd be fine. For now, Mama had to lie down.

The left side of my face was puffed out like a chipmunk's. I followed all of the doctor's instructions and elevated my head and took more Tylenol to minimize bruising. The next day I took off my bandages. The side of my face was still very swollen, and I was finding it hard to talk. I couldn't drink or chew properly. Well, maybe that might help me lose a few pounds too? (Bright side?) I had the email of my doctor's assistant and typed:

"Hi there. Just wanted to know if it's normal that one side of my face is very swollen and it's really challenging to talk. Could you ask the doctor?"

She emailed back and said to send some pictures, one smiling, one normal, and one with a pursed mouth like I was pouting. My bottom lip looked like it had vanished. My smile was lopsided. I started looking stuff up on the Internet.

Yikes. Close the computer.

Then I looked at the possible side effects on the sheets I had initialed before the procedure. Fourth one down: Nerve injury. Marginal mandibular nerve palsy. Inability to depress lower lip. Temporary change in smile or facial expression. Yes, this looked like what

I might be experiencing. I was mad at myself. Why hadn't I read the fine print? Why had I glossed over these many side effects without asking questions? How many times do we glance through pages of paperwork without fully reading it and nonchalantly sign on the dotted line? I should've asked more questions before I had this done, and more importantly before I signed the paperwork.

I made an appointment to see the doctor who performed the Fractora procedure a few days later. I took Sean, who was trying to hold back his anger.

My first question was "Will it come back?" And he said yes, 100 percent.

How long before I went from zero to 100 percent?

He admitted he wasn't sure. Maybe a few weeks. He asked if he could try to even out my mouth with a little Botox, and I could mask some of it with makeup.

Ummmm—what about the fact that I can't speak certain words? And my lopsided smile? There was no way I could go back on the air looking like this.

I was near tears. This was not what I had signed up for, dammit. Sean asked the doctor what percentage of patients this happened to. He said about 1 to 2 percent. Ugh.

I went to work the following week even though I was lisping, and mistakenly I tried going on the air.

I did one weather report at 5:00 a.m. for *Fox & Friends* first, but I sounded drunk. I could feel my lopsided mouth, and it felt worse because when I'm on television, I project a little bigger with words and expressions. It was even harder to enunciate. I started to panic while on the air. I knew I had to wrap this weather report quickly, so I just turned my head and my body to the left, so you could just see one side of my face, the good side, facing the camera. I quickly said "Back to you" and didn't smile like I usually do when I toss back to the anchors.

I was mortified. Embarrassed. Sad. And then ashamed.

Why had I been so vain to do this to myself?

I emailed my bosses Lauren Petterson and Suzanne Scott, president of programming, and admitted to them what had happened. Suzanne asked to see a couple of screen grabs from the weather report I had done to see what I was referring to. I couldn't look at them. They were both so kind and told me to go home, rest up, we would take it day by day.

I went home and spent another week off the air. In between, I was sending my doctor pictures of my face for him to look at. And then I went for a second opinion with another plastic surgeon because I was so nervous about why this was taking so long to heal.

The second-opinion doc took pictures and told me to try and show my bottom teeth. I couldn't. He asked me to do a few more exercises, which I also couldn't perform. I then started to feel like maybe this could be permanent. I knew my lip had to be trembling as tears came to my eyes, but I couldn't feel my mouth.

His conclusion after the office exam was that I might not be back to normal in six months; it might take a year. He was hopeful that the damage wasn't permanent, but he told me the other doctor had heated up the facial nerve and it was swollen. It would take time to get back to normal, and only time was going to help it.

I was also scared that the MS and terrible immune system might be the reason why the healing was taking so long. I made an appointment to see my neurologist, and she concluded the MS was NOT to blame. I told her I was embarrassed about what I had done, and she was sympathetic. She said I shouldn't be ashamed. Every woman feels the pressure to look younger, even in professions that don't have a camera following them.

I emailed my mom when she asked me why she wasn't seeing me in the morning and told her what had happened.

She wrote back and said:

"Please don't feel shame. I would do it too!"

Many people were telling me to enjoy those weeks off work to relax, get some rest, and spend time with my family. Every day I was looking at my face in the mirror and stressing out that I might never get my smile back. Not having my big, toothy grin was spiraling me into a deep depression.

I had another panic attack several weeks after another visit to my doctor, who was still telling me I would be back to normal any day now. Although, in one of his last emails before I decided I could never go back to him again, he told me he was "praying and meditating for the universe to help make things better."

Not exactly what you want to hear from a plastic surgeon.

"Why does he keep telling me it's coming back? I don't think it's *ever* coming back!" I yelled at my husband.

I was depressed, sad, and ashamed. I lost weight and was inconsolable at times.

My childhood friend Neera, who has been one of my closest girlfriends for over twenty-five years, came to spend a night with me in New York. We were planning to go out to dinner and catch up, have fun on the town. I was so upset about my crooked smile and being off work that we just ended up spending the night in the hotel lobby having drinks. She was sweet and understanding. She listened to me and offered advice and reminded me I could always move back to Canada and resume my radio career, where I wouldn't have all this pressure on me. Mostly she was just there to be a comforting presence in a dark time.

Another week went by, and I was getting a lot of messages on social media asking where I was. I didn't know what to say. Many people thought I was off because of an MS relapse. I couldn't just address what had happened in a tweet or on Facebook.

Gradually, I started feeling more comfortable admitting to people what had happened to me: what was supposed to be a somewhat simple outpatient procedure turned into a nightmare. As I told my story, many women (and men) were telling me stories about themselves or people they knew who had experienced unwanted side effects or setbacks from cosmetic procedures or surgery.

And then I realized that maybe if I shared my story I might be able to help others. I had done it with MS; why should it be any different talking about Fractora?

I emailed Lauren and Suzanne to ask if they were open to me coming back to *Fox & Friends* and talking about what happened. They agreed that if it was something I wanted to do, they were behind me 100 percent. Plus, it might get me back on air sooner.

I started writing about the experience of being sidelined after what was supposed to be an easy neck procedure as an op-ed for Foxnews.com. I wrote about how many of us don't talk about what we do with our faces and bodies because we live in a society where we are all supposed to look healthy, beautiful, and young naturally. No one wants to admit to going under the knife or doing something to their face or body to look better. However, I didn't want to feel shame for what I did or embarrassment about wanting to look better.

I sent it to Lynne Jordal Martin, a senior editor at Foxnews.com, who is also a good friend and confidante. She wrote me right back:

My dear wonderful Janice!!
I have been wondering about you and missing you on

air—and I am a jumble of emotions right now. I think this is GREAT. And so honest. As always, your honesty and candor are so incredible. I think this would help a lot of women. It's that powerful.

Big, HUGE hug to you. And another. If you are in the office today, I will come up and visit you to deliver the hug in person.

Love you,
Lynne

Feeling a little more confident, I decided to get another opinion from my friend Megyn Kelly.

She always gives it to me straight as a girlfriend and as someone who also happens to be in this wacky business.

JD:

Your essay is excellent. I think there is some downside to disclosing this—namely, some will revel in it, it will call attention to something you feel insecure about, and it will be attached to you if you are open about the situation.

The upside is probably far greater, however. You will receive enormous support—way more support and love than criticism. You might help someone. You will get yourself back on the air (although here again you run the risk of someone doing a daily or weekly "Janice Dean's face" update, which might be upsetting, or perhaps you will easily laugh that off).

When you get back on air, maybe they can shoot you from farther back, so it's not such a tight angle. Like the outdoor weather stuff you sometimes do. Also, start doing very dramatic eyes and neutral lips—that may help.

But, having said all that, you have always been open and

sharing, and that has worked to your benefit—mostly b/c it's who you are—it's authentic. I think women would only love you more for the disclosure, some men too, and it might help you psychologically in getting past what is a difficult—albeit temporary—situation.

And finally, what you wrote, if you decide to disclose, is perfect. I wouldn't change a word (except to proof it). You're so honest and so relatable, and every reader will be rooting for you and will be as upset as you are at the outcome. No one on earth can realistically question any choice you have made, and it does sound an important warning for all of us about how these risks are not just legal disclosures.

I love you JD. And I'm sorry you are going thru this. And I will be there right next to you in spirit (and defending you publicly) and physically across the table from you with a vat of wine if you decide to put it out there.

MK

Full disclosure: there may have been a few lunches with a vat of wine in front of us while I was off work with my bum lip.

After talking it over with Sean, I decided I wanted to share my experience with others, so I published the op-ed and titled it: "Always Read the Fine Print. The Last Two Months Have Been a Real PAIN IN THE NECK."

It was published the day I went back to *Fox & Friends* where I sat down with my friend Ainsley Earhardt and talked about the procedure, what it was like being off for two months, and the shame and embarrassment I went through.

The opinion piece resonated. It had over a million views. I did interviews with women's magazines and talked about it on some of our local Fox affiliates. Many women shared their cosmetic stories or told me that now they were rethinking some of these new "miracle lunchtime tune-ups." I remember one day I was sitting in the makeup chair, having just been back for a week or so. A makeup artist who had just started at Fox asked me if she could give me a hug. She whispered in my ear: "My mom loves you and is so glad you're back. She sent me your article and told me she thinks every woman should read it. Thank you for being so 'real.'"

I cried. And she had to reapply my makeup.

Here's what I've learned: These new lasers, injections, and cosmetic procedures that look as if they can turn back time? There's a little more to it. There are risks. It takes a while to heal. It's also expensive. There are many possible complications that we need to be aware of before we sign on the dotted line. We should ask our doctors about the worst-case scenario, so we're prepared.

I wish we women wouldn't put so much pressure on ourselves. I have a little group of women I text on a daily basis. We call ourselves the "sorority." Most of us are in television, and we gossip about the sometimes unforgiving business we're in. We all talk about our aging faces and bodies and get advice from one another about what to do to hide our muffin tops, our gray hair, and the latest in skin care. I think we all need to love and support each other when it comes to aging gracefully. Especially in a forum where we are in many ways judged by our appearance.

I've since asked many people what they don't like about themselves. And more often than not, they tell me their biggest flaw is something I never would've guessed.

We're the harshest critics of ourselves.

My husband, Sean, once told me about a science fiction story he had read when he was in college about a time traveler who went into the future where everyone looked young and perfect. The traveler was aging normally—with wrinkles and a face and body that appeared much older than everyone else in this place he was visiting. And guess what happened? He became beautiful to all of them. And they wanted to look like he did.

I do believe that beauty comes from within. I've met many pretty faces who were not nice people, and all of a sudden they weren't attractive anymore. No amount of makeup or facetuning can cover up an ugly personality.

We spend too much time focused on our self-perceived flaws instead of embracing the things that make us all shine. After I was back at work for a few months after the Fractora incident my husband commented that he caught me smiling at my kids without being self-conscious. For weeks I had been smiling less or covering my mouth to hide it. Now my big smile was coming back! Tears sprang to my eyes. You know what? My kids couldn't care less about what my neck looks like. When they see their mama smiling big and wide, that's what they remember most.

That's what I'm going to try and focus on when I look in the mirror. Or, better yet, less time in front of the mirror and more time seeing my reflection in my beautiful kids' faces.

Chapter 19

STANDING UP TO
ONLINE TROLLS

As you've figured out, I am pretty open when it comes to my life behind the scenes, away from the camera, microphone, and bright lights. When I went back to work after the home invasion in Houston, I decided to go on the air during my morning show to talk about what happened because I figured I might be able to help someone else, and for me, talking about it helps me process traumatic events. I did the same with my MS diagnosis and the Fractora neck nightmare. Many people have told me not to be so public when it comes to personal issues, but I feel it has helped me connect with others, which is why many of us get into television in the first place. I remember watching Oprah in my teens and twenties, and although I couldn't tell you the exact episodes that touched me the most, what I remember was how open and honest she was about her struggles with weight and events that had happened in her personal life that made us believe she could be our friend even though we had never met her. There are not too many others who have done that in the world of broadcasting.

Of course, being honest about life experiences can leave you a little more vulnerable. Even before the world of social media, I would receive emails from viewers saying some pretty mean stuff. With the invention of Twitter, Facebook, and Instagram, it's open season for criticism from people who can be somewhat anonymous. I enjoy the MUTE button on Twitter a great deal because people can comment all day long and THINK I might be reading their ideas and suggestions but in reality I never see them on my timeline. A lot of people use BLOCK to avoid the rude and sometimes obscene commentary, but many of these trolls take great pride in being blocked by someone and will use it as a badge of honor. They'll even list it in their bio: "I WAS BLOCKED BY ——! I TROLLED THEM SO MUCH THEY COULDN'T TAKE IT ANYMORE, SUCKER!"

Muting is much more satisfying in my opinion because it's just like ignoring the bully. And then of course if something is mean or X-rated, you can ask Twitter to ban them from the ranting and raving, but that may only last a week or two and then they're back to their old tricks. Muting is the way to go. It's like turning the noise off on the loud, mean comments.

Instagram is not nearly as harsh as Twitter and Facebook. There are occasionally inappropriate remarks, but Instagram is mainly for pictures, and there don't seem to be as many outspoken followers who yell at your dog or cute baby pictures.

I have a personal Facebook page under my married name where I only accept close friends and family. And then I have my Fox Facebook page, which I've had for over a decade. I post pictures from *Fox & Friends* and mostly work-related articles and pictures on the job. I will peruse some of the comments and respond when I can. Sometimes there are mean remarks that I will ignore, but once in a blue moon I have to catch my breath and react. This is what happened with a person named "JoAnn" under a photo of me smiling while reporting outside in the snow. (Who knew a hat with a pom-pom could trigger such an outburst!)

Dear Janice, please stop allowing fox to dress you in those short skirts. They are not flattering on you. Your an attractive lady, love the 80's hair, but your legs are distracting every time you walk on the screen.

Right away it felt cruel. She didn't swear or call me names, but it was shameful to me. Maybe others would've reacted differently or ignored it, but this one had neon lights around it. I read it again. And then I wrote her back:

Fox doesn't dress me. I dress myself. I'm sorry if you don't like my legs. I'm grateful to have them to walk with. You're right. I don't look like the typical person on TV, and I'm proud to be a size 10. Imagine that! You can always turn the channel if you're offended by my huge legs. Hope you don't mind. I may share your post with everyone on my FB page.

JoAnn must've been monitoring her Facebook comments, because she responded immediately. This time she bit back and told me I need to be *careful*. I could lose my job at any time. I'm *older* now. There's a new regime now at Fox. A much younger, thinner, prettier reporter could easily move into my role. I fired back that it was interesting that she knew so much considering she wasn't in media. She slammed back: "You know nothing about me!" I raised my eyebrows. And said to myself: *JoAnn you, know nothing about me either.*

Now, for every mean comment, there will be ten of them that are kind and sweet. I have many defenders on my Faccbook page who are complete strangers. But one name that popped up on the JoAnn timeline was a familiar one. It was from my friend Jen Smrtka, my MS nurse practitioner who had worked with Dr. Tullman when I was newly diagnosed. She wrote:

> Dear Janice. I LOVE those strong legs. I LOVE that you stand tall, walk, run, squat, lunge, skip, jump and hop on those legs. You are so blessed and a blessing to have STRONG legs. Wear skirts proudly and show your STRONG legs! Love you, my angel.

And then the tears came. A reminder that no matter what size or shape they are, our legs should be celebrated and not be taken for granted. One of the things I've been very conscious of after being diagnosed with MS is that I could, at any time, lose the use of my legs. Nerve damage from MS can reduce your ability to move and perform everyday activities. Our muscles can tire more easily, and our legs can feel unstable or we can have trouble moving them. Sometimes MS affects the muscles of the foot making it hard to walk normally, and as a result our feet drag on the ground. So, yes, my big, strong legs were something to be grateful for, not to be ashamed of.

Over the years after my MS diagnosis, I've tried hard to not sweat the small stuff after being so focused on career goals and overachieving.

I've been every size from a 4 to a 12. At times I was unhealthy and lost weight to look "good." And now I've comfortably settled into a size 10(-ish)—that's an average, by the way—and you ladies know what I'm talking about. I'm a 6 to 8 on top (torso), but on the bottom (thighs, butt) I'm a 10 to 12. But, depending on the designer or the clothing maker, we fluctuate. It's ridiculous and maddening.

If you look around the TV landscape, size 10(-ish) is large in my world. I'm in a sea of size 0 to 4 dresses. And I think that's a bit sad, since it does not represent the general population outside of the screen people see us on. It used to bother me, but now I kind of take pride in the fact that I'm different.

I do wish the industry I'm in would change, though. I'd like to see more of me on TV. I still feel a shiver of shame when I go to wardrobe events at work where there are dresses in every color, but out of one hundred of them, only one or two will fit me. I've had wardrobe personnel make plenty of comments over the years about my size bringing me right back to my teenage self in the husky girls department. I've had them say in front of me, "You can't wear that dress. That would never fit over your hips." And I've had them say to someone right next to me, "You're my favorite size. A perfect size zero!! It's a pleasure to find clothes for you!" while I stand there with a red face.

Many of us in television have wardrobe allowances in our contracts. For many years I felt too self-conscious to go to what they call trunk shows every season to try on dresses that the wardrobe department would purchase for us. I knew from experience there would never be much selection for me. My friend Jane Skinner told me she felt the same way and would never use all of her clothing allowance either. Jane was never overweight, but she also wasn't a size 0. We both concluded that if it was our money, we should be able to use it. If the wardrobe people didn't get things that fit us, then why shouldn't we buy it ourselves and be reimbursed? That's what I do now: I go shopping on my own and put dresses, skirts, and suits aside so that I spend my allowance that is owed to me in my contract. I may be in the minority, but that doesn't mean I shouldn't be able to dress nicely and look just as nice as my size 2 colleagues.

I've been bullied about my appearance on and off my whole life, from grade school to *Imus*, to even when I was eight months pregnant.

All of these came flooding back after that Facebook post from "JoAnn." In that moment, it was clear I had to stand up for myself. And since then, I've had many coworkers come up and hug me. A cameraman who popped his head into my office to tell me that his sister and mom were proud of me—and so was he. A neighbor whom I haven't seen in a while motioned me to roll down my window while I waited to pick up my son at school to say, "Good for you!" I've had emails from friends and strangers who wanted to express their support. It touched a nerve for not just me but many others who read and identified with the pushback from an online bully.

I think from a wider lens this is all part of a larger movement—a kind of #metoo moment when it comes to bullying or shaming someone. Right now, we feel more empowered to call out behavior that feels wrong.

And I think that's why that one Facebook comment and reply went viral. It's a reminder to the JoAnns and all the bullies in the schoolyard past and present. It's not funny or nice to pass judgment on someone until you've walked in their shoes.

And to the women out there who want to get into television or a world where appearances seem hard to achieve, let me give you some advice that's worked for me: Be yourself. Show them who you are. Be proud of your shape and size, because I am standing up for you, too—on my big, strong legs!

Chapter 20

FLARE-UP

On the first day of third grade, my son Matthew came home to tell me his teacher, Mrs. Klein, was in a wheelchair. She said it was important for her kids to see her working like everyone else despite being in a wheelchair. I asked Matthew what he thought of that.

"I think she's the coolest teacher I've ever had."

Did she say why she was in a wheelchair?

"She said she had something called MS."

At that moment I realized I had never really told my two boys I have multiple sclerosis. They knew I had to have injections to make me "feel better," but not exactly why. Now I had to tell Matthew and his brother, Theodore, that I had the same thing as Mrs. Klein. Matthew's eyes got wider.

"Will you be in a wheelchair?"

I said I didn't know. It was possible. Would that matter?

"No," he said. "Mrs. Klein is awesome!"

Theodore said maybe he could sit on my lap and we could race on the wheelchair. I emailed Mrs. Klein that night. It was early in the school year, and she wanted all the parents to write a little something about her students so she could get to know them. I took this as a perfect opportunity to introduce myself and let her know she had just given me a tremendous gift:

Hi Mrs. Klein,

First, let me start by saying we are thrilled you are Matthew's third-grade teacher. We've heard such excellent things from other parents. I asked Matthew how he likes his class and he grinned and said he "loves it." This is so wonderful. We are grateful to start off the school year with happy boys. Our other son Theodore said you met him in the hallway today and had a nice chat.

I must admit—we forgot to put the student planner in Matthew's book bag last week and today. It will be in his backpack from now on.

A few things about our son Matthew. He is a good boy. He's kind and sensitive (it doesn't take much to get him upset— he's like his mom. Tears can come easily). He gets along with others. He can be influenced a little bit by his friends, but he listens to authority and will correct behavior when asked to. He loves school and enjoys all subjects. Please let me know if there's anything you need us to do to help him along in his studies or work on with him.

One other thing I wanted to add. Matthew told us you discussed having MS with the class. I have MS too. I was diagnosed over 10 years ago, and while I've never told the boys exactly what I have, they know I have to take medicine and sometimes sleep more than they do. They also know I can't be outside in the hot sun for a long time. Today I was able to tell them both I have the same thing Mrs. Klein has. It brought tears to my eyes because you opened the door for me to be honest with them and name the illness that's remained a bit of a secret. I am so grateful. I'm a bit teary right now as I type this. Both my boys were talking about MS tonight and were fascinated that I had the same thing as Mrs. Klein.

Thank you for being such an excellent role model for your students, and for me.

Janice

She wrote back:

Hi Mrs. Dean,

First, I must say that your email brought tears to my eyes, as well. Matthew (and Theodore) are wonderful boys, and I was touched to see their reaction when seeing each other in the hallway. It was truly very sweet. All that you expressed about Matthew appears quite true in class, but it is always special to see what parents have to say about their children at the beginning of the year.

As for sharing about your MS, your words really touched my heart. Aside from my love of teaching, one of the reasons I have persisted in my career is because I hoped to show children, by example, that when life gets you down, you pick yourself up and move on . . .

MS is such a curious disease with such a broad range of symptoms. I will be sure to mention that to the children this year as well. I was diagnosed 20 years ago, and the wheelchair became necessary about 15 years later. It is so great to see how well you are doing and that no one would ever suspect a struggle. Oddly enough, I never experience the fatigue that is so common in MS—Further proof that MS can take random and different paths in every patient. May we both continue in relatively good health and positive spirits. I look forward to working with the entire family this year.

JK

I do believe people come into our lives for a reason. Mrs. Klein was not only a fantastic teacher, she provided a beautiful opening for me to introduce my kids to the illness I will have probably for the rest of my life. I am forever grateful to her. My boys will sometimes ask questions about the disease, but I encourage them to talk about it with me and ask everything they need to. I never want them to be shy or scared to discuss it. I remind them I'm taking my medicine, I'm staying healthy, and I'm going to try and be around for a long, long time.

It's hard to believe it's been almost fourteen years since my first MS episode. There are ongoing reminders that my immune system isn't the greatest, and I do know that this illness remains unpredictable—much like the weather I forecast—and can strike when you least expect it.

There were many years where the disease was somewhat dormant, but last year I had a harsh reminder it was still lurking.

After receiving my latest round of MRIs, my neurologist, Dr. DeAngelis, called me at home. I was sitting at the kitchen table with my neighbor Dervla and Sean, having tea and leftover donuts from my son Theodore's seventh birthday. The phone buzzed, and Dr. DeAngelis's number came up. I had been waiting for a week or so for the results of the three separate rounds of tests. She had them.

"Hi, Janice. Sorry to bother you at home on a Friday night."

"No problem, Dr. DeAngelis." I got up from the table. My husband nodded at me like he knew I had to go into the other room.

"So your MRIs came back. Your brain is clear. But I see new activity on your spine."

I felt a punch in my gut.

I hadn't had any new lesions on my spine in years.

She named the exact sections on my spine she saw these new spots.

"Janice, I think it's time we get more aggressive. Are you open to a different therapy? We just did your bloodwork, and you are a good candidate for a drug called Tysabri. Have you heard of it?"

I told her I had. I remembered that there was a low risk of a brain disease that could potentially kill a person.

She told me that, yes, there is a less than 1 in 10,000 person risk you could get PML (short for progressive multifocal leukoencephalopathy), but that they would monitor me closely while on the drug and the minute they saw any changes in my bloodwork or my behavior they would take me off it. The upside of the drug was tremendous, and many MS patients love being on it. Instead of an injection every day or three times a week, it was an infusion once a month when I went to their office, and it would take two hours. That was it. The maintenance was easy, and the efficacy of this drug had been very good since it was introduced on the market when it came to relapsing-remitting MS. The vast majority of us MS club members have relapsing-remitting MS (RRMS). This means there are periods of active inflammation in the central nervous system (brain/spine), and during that time symptoms worsen and new symptoms may develop. With RRMS, there are times when the symptoms are less pronounced. The quiet periods between relapses are called remissions; remissions can last months or years. In my case it's been years since I've had anything to report or show up on my MRI scans.

Dr. DeAngelis reassured me that I was young (I love her for saying this), active, and doing great. Even if this new drug helped keep my immune system from gnawing away at my central nervous system for a year or two before I potentially went on something else, it might be worth trying.

(Just a side note here for those of you who have MS and are reading this: I am not endorsing any kind of MS therapy. All I know is the drug that I was taking on and off for thirteen years wasn't working for me, and it was time to try something else.)

Having an illness like MS is so personal. It's hard to talk about it with people who don't have it. The same can be said for those who go through any other kind of health issue. There's a fine line you walk when you talk to people outside of your family and doctors. Some people are terrific, like my neighbor Dervla. When I got back to the kitchen after talking to Dr. DeAngelis, I was shaking. Dervla has known about my MS, but she's never really asked me about it that much. She takes cues from me on whether or not I want to talk about it. I told her and Sean what the doctor had just said over the phone.

Sean went to the fridge and asked if we wanted to switch from tea to a bottle of wine.

Bless my husband. He opened the pinot grigio.

I filled them in on what was going on, the risks, the new lesions, how scary this all was again. I was doing so well, and now a setback. It goes right back to what I said earlier about this crummy disease. Like a thunderstorm, you know it's possible, but you can never time the lightning or the crash of noise.

I emailed my fellow MS buddy Neil Cavuto down the hallway at Fox:

Hi Neil,

My doc says she wants to try Tysabri on me. I've had a few new spots on my spine, and she thinks this may be a better therapy. Have you tried this my friend? If you don't mind, I'm going to pop my head into your office this week.

JD

Neil wrote back:

I have not, Janice, but I have heard good things . . . stop by any
time. By the way, nice exchange with those Brazilian tourists
the other day on tv!
Hugs,
Neil

A few days later I was at work. Admittedly this was not my best
week at the office. I was tired, irritable, and thinking about the damn
MS and the new drug. I was also questioning why this was happening
again. Had I done something different? Was I stressed-out more than
usual? Not getting enough rest? It was weighing on my mind heavily.

A colleague who has a loved one living with MS was at work the
week I was getting this crappy news. He started chatting with me
about an MS fund-raising event that was coming up and asked if I
was interested in taking part. Normally, I don't mind, but this week I
didn't want to, and I should've said that right away when he brought
it up. I told him I had just seen my doctor and I was having a flare-up.
Maybe I thought he would be sympathetic, and we could bad-mouth
MS together, but instead of a therapy session, it got me upset.

This person immediately asked me what drug I was taking. I told
him I was on Copaxone. Was I on the daily injection or the three-days-
a-week? I told him the three-days-a-week. He told me his thoughts on
the difference between the daily and the three-days-a-week.

I was irritated, and I told him I was thinking of trying something
else. (Dumb move!) He then asked me what drug and I told him.
(UGH!)

"Tysabri."

He launched into a speech about all the bad stuff he had heard
about the drug.

He reminded me that because he had a person close to him who was living with MS, he had done his research when it came to treatments and detection. Not only that, but he "felt" the emotion that comes with living with a person who has it.

He was MS'plaining.

Not only did this person question the therapy my doctor and I were deciding on, but he also told me that I should wait and get another opinion, perhaps one in a different state. In fact, while we were on the subject, maybe it was time to go to a different place for my MRIs. Some places don't calibrate their machines, and the findings could be wrong. If I had been a cartoon, there would have been steam coming out of my ears.

My blood pressure was going through the roof, and I tried to make excuses as to why I had to leave this conversation abruptly and barely made it to my office without breaking down.

I slammed the door. Didn't he get it?

I clenched my fists trying to calm down.

I called my husband to vent. As soon as he answered the phone, I broke down in tears—the hyperventilating kind of tears where Sean can't understand a word I'm saying.

He was able to piece together enough despite my bawling, sniffling, and stuttering and told me some people just don't get it. It wasn't anybody's business except ours how we were planning to manage this.

I called my beloved Nurse Practitioner Jen. She was calm and also assured me it was none of anyone's concern what my treatment was or is. Everyone's MS is different. It's between you and your doctor. No one else's opinion helps much.

I was so angry. So angry. I was upset for much of the weekend.

The colleague ended up apologizing many times. Now that I'm in a calmer place, I realize he was just trying to help.

My dear friend Meghan McCain, who was with her father, Sena-

tor John McCain, during his diagnosis and his treatment with ter-
minal brain cancer, said something that brought me to tears. We
were talking about my new medicine I was about to go on. She
asked what it entailed, and I told her I would have to go to a doctor's office and get an infusion. She said these simple words: "Can
I come and keep you company? I know how scary and lonely that
stuff can be." That was all she needed to say for me to feel like I was
loved and cared for by a friend. She continues to ask me when my
next infusion is—every time she sees me—and wants to come the
next time I go. I always tell her she doesn't physically need to be by
my side. I feel her presence right there. I love her so much.

My hero Neil Cavuto never fails to remind me his door is always
open to talk about the disease we share and how we're both hanging in.

And just as Neil did for me over a decade ago, I got a reminder that
by going public with my illness, I've helped others too.

It was National Grilled Cheese Day. (If you haven't already realized, I have designated myself as the official *Fox & Friends* ambassador
for all food-related holidays.) We had a 70-pound homemade grilled
cheese sandwich out on the street: 50 pounds of Velveeta cheese,
10 pounds of butter, and two giant homemade pieces of bread that
weighed 5 pounds each. I carved myself a healthy portion for my own
personal taste test, and, as predicted, it was delicious. Afterward, I
was in the green room when one of the gentlemen who helped put
together these 70 pounds of goodness came up to me. I shook his
hand and told him how grateful I was for the cheesy great morning
snack, when he whispered:

"Thank you for being open about your MS. My wife was just diagnosed. I was so touched by what I've read and seen about how you've
used your diagnosis to help people."

I kept his hand in mine after the handshake and asked about his
wife and how she was doing. He admitted it had been very scary, and

they were still in a world of shock. He confessed he didn't know who I was when he was asked to come and be a part of the on-air segment but had googled my name beforehand and saw I had the same illness as his wife. When he saw I was still working despite the illness and enjoying giant grilled cheese sandwiches, it made him—and his wife—feel less alone.

I told him to take my phone number and my email and give it to his wife. I said I would be happy to talk to her anytime about what she's dealing with and be a soundingboard. I could see in his eyes that this man was so in love, but he felt helpless and just wanted to take her fear and pain away. After spending a few minutes with him discussing different therapies and reassuring him that she would be okay, I felt I had at least cleared away a few little storm clouds in his mind. Sometimes it just takes one person and a kind word to make you feel less alone when it comes to this frustrating illness.

A day later, I was doing weather outside and had a good little crowd of people behind me waving to the camera and telling me all about their hometowns. After my report, a man took my hand with tears in his eyes and told me his wife had just been newly diagnosed with MS. I asked him how she was doing, and he confided that they were both scared of the road ahead—but that he wanted to tell me how grateful he was that I had opened up about my journey. He politely asked what medication I was taking, and I told him the name of the new drug I was on and said I was feeling some side effects. Still, I was optimistic about our future. He asked for a hug, and I gave him one and told him I would pray for his wife and send good vibes her way. I was crying now. Both of these men came into my life and reaffirmed that I was somehow helping others.

A few weeks later I got an email from a woman named Nicole. Here's what she wrote:

Hi Janice,

I hope this finds you well. My husband, Justin, met you recently at a *Fox & Friends* filming and passed along your contact information to me. I wanted to reiterate his thanks for using your platform to raise awareness about MS.

It has been just over 2 years since my diagnosis, and I still struggle to process this part of me. Each person's journey is unique, but your words resonate deeply with me on this sometimes-lonely path. Like you, I feel gratitude for things that once seemed mundane. I thank my legs for carrying me forward to new and familiar places, my eyes for allowing me to observe this beautiful and complicated world, and my dear husband, who embraces life's uncertainties beside me.

Sometimes I worry that this new reality will just break Justin's giant and gentle heart. I see how he feels my pain from these damn injections and how frustrated he feels by our lack of control over all of this. But when he came back from New York, I could also see his optimism and determination to continue building our beautiful life.

Thank you, Janice, for your generosity of self. Your voice reaches millions and raises important awareness about this invisible illness that affects so many people around the world, and especially at home in Canada. And more personally, your voice reached my husband and me when we needed to hear it. I am truly grateful.

Sending much love and strength to you and your army of support. You've got this!

With love,

Nicole

I am still so glad I was open and honest from the beginning about sharing my journey with MS. We're all just doing the best we can. We need to remind ourselves that you never know what battle someone might be fighting. Sometimes the best medicine is to just be kind.

By the way, the new drugs I'm on have been great. I had a bumpy ride in the beginning, and another big flare-up, but lately I've been feeling like myself. Perhaps even better. I still have to get tests to make sure I'm still a good candidate for the Tysabri. They look for a virus that could make me more susceptible to the brain disease. While this is scary, the benefits of the drug are so far outweighing that small possibility of the worst-case scenario. Having MS is a very good reminder to try to live life to the fullest. MS = Mostly Sunny. Not sweating the small stuff and looking for silver linings.

There are so many different therapies out there for us MS'ers. Every time I see my doctor, she tells me they are getting very close to major breakthroughs. Once they crack the code of MS, it will help doctors to understand the building blocks of other neurological illnesses. I am optimistic that the forecast is looking sunnier for us.

And, I do believe there will be a day soon when having MS will no longer be associated with wheelchairs.

But until then, like my friend Mrs. Klein says:

"When life gets you down, you pick yourself up and move on . . ."

Chapter 21

WHERE THE SKIES ARE SO BLUE

One of the lessons I've learned in my life is to live in the moment. If you ever get the chance to do something you've always wanted to do, you need to take the wheel and start driving. I've had a lot of reminders in my life that life is short, and we need to enjoy the sunshine. I know that sounds clichéd, but over the last few years I've tried to do things that put a little skip in my step and remind me that I'm still alive and kicking. Luckily, I'm in a job that allows me to dream big, and if the opportunity arises, a camera will follow me.

Giddy-Up!

One of those moments is the Kentucky Derby at Churchill Downs. I absolutely love this assignment and have done it two years in a row. It's all about dressing up, drinking mint juleps, and showing off your best Derby hats. In the sporting world, it's the oldest continuously held major event in the United States. Did I say I get to wear pretty hats?

The night before the Derby there's a huge event that's been happening for three decades called the Barnstable Brown Gala in which celebrities and musicians come to the Barnstable Brown twin sisters' home and raise money for charity. There's a big red-carpet event before the party, and we get some fun clips from all the familiar faces attending the event.

A couple of years ago Harry Connick Jr. was singing the national anthem, and he was there with his wife and daughters. I shouted his name as he was walking the carpet, and he came over to talk to us. So, Harry Connick is a pretty swoon-worthy fella. One of my girlfriends who shall remain nameless calls him her imaginary husband (even though she's happily married to a real-life awesome guy). I asked Mr. Connick if he could sing a few bars of "The Star-Spangled Banner" for the *Fox & Friends* viewers but he politely declined. I then asked if perhaps he could sing a few lines of "Happy Birthday," since my birthday is just a few days after the Derby. He smiled, and I think I even caught a little sparkle in his eye as he said:

"How about a kiss instead?"

I think my whole face went flush with excitement, and I managed to respond with:

"Uhhhhh . . . ARE YOU KIDDING ME?"

While I was fangirling out, somehow my reporter instincts took over and made sure I turned my face toward the TV camera and got him to plant his pucker right on my cheek for all the world to witness. There were flashbulbs popping and photos were taken.

It should also be noted that his wife and daughters were looking over his shoulder with a few interesting glances while the camera was rolling. This, my friends, was an I-have-the-best-job-in-the-world moment. There's life before Harry Connick Jr. kisses your cheek and life afterward. My husband even told me this was huge. He mentioned that some of his firefighter buddies called him after they saw the moment on television and one guy confessed that Harry Connick Jr. was his wife's "hall pass."

The following year a reporter at the Derby came up to me and said, "You're the one Harry kissed! You're a legend!"

Back to reality. What were we talking about?

Oh, yes, horse racing.

Sean and I had one of our first dates at Belmont Park racetrack back in 2003. Sean and his friend Tommy went to the track for many years, and back when we first started dating he thought it might be a fun New York thing for us to do. It ended up raining the day of the famous Belmont Stakes, and Sean had to pick me up and carry me over some of the enormous puddles, since I was not dressed appropriately: I was wearing fancy high-heeled sandals. The part about Sean lifting me over puddles was romantic; the rest of the day was not. I talked about my trip to the racetrack on *Imus* the following day and mentioned how horrible the experience was, getting wet and cold. I don't even remember watching the races, but with wet frizzy hair and flooded shoes when I was trying to impress Sean. Nothing else mattered.

I announced on air that I was out at Belmont with friends, and it was not the Seabiscuit experience I was hoping for. Imus thought this was funny, and I could tell he wanted me to emphasize how awful it was, so I embellished quite a bit while avoiding talking about being on a date with Sean. The track was terrible, getting there was a pain in the ass, and the clientele were drunk and unruly. Plus, my cute outfit ended up soaking wet and I smelled like a wet horse when I got home. As luck would have it, the head of the National Thoroughbred Racing Association (NTRA) was a big Imus fan and was horrified listening to my experience.

He called one of his young employees, Pete Rotondo, to send me the biggest flower arrangement possible while writing on the sympathy card how the racing community would like to treat me to a weekend at Saratoga to make up for my soggy-wet racetrack experience. I accepted the offer and whispered into the phone, asking if I could bring my "friend" Sean and his buddy Tommy to Saratoga. It ended up being one of the best weekends I've ever had. It did change my mind about horse racing. We were up in the fancy seats, hanging out with some big New York mucky-mucks, eating shrimp cocktail and drinking fancy cocktails.

It was also one of my first romantic trips with Sean, so that was a definite bonus. The other big draw was wearing a fancy hat, something that has become a tradition of mine. The bigger the hat, the better. So when I got to go to the Derby over a decade later, and witness two Triple Crowns at Belmont with Sean and his buddy Tommy at the same place we shared one of our first dates, it goes down as a top-ten moment. And, to prove you just never know who might show up in life later, Peter Rotondo, the fella who bought me the flowers and showed me around Saratoga, is now VP of the Breeders' Cup and is a guest on *Fox & Friends* every year to talk about how to place your bets at the Derby. I like to brag to him that he's known me as long as I've known my husband and to date has given me the biggest, baddest bouquet of roses I have ever received.

The Triple Crown is the biggest achievement a horse can have in its career. They start with the Derby. Then they head to the Preakness in Baltimore, and if they win both of those races, they head to Belmont Park in New York for a shot at the Triple Crown. It's the longest race at 1.5 miles and the crown is one of the most elusive titles in sports.

Only thirteen horses have won the Triple Crown since 1875 in spite of the three races needed to win.

American Pharoah did it in 2015 (after thirty-seven years without a Triple Crown winner) and Justify won again in 2018. Last year I interviewed the world-famous jockey Mike Smith, who was riding Justify; Bob Baffert, Justify's trainer; and one of the owners of the horse, Sol Kumin. That doesn't happen very often: to get to interview all of these people before such a huge race. My producer Sam and I knew it was the Triple Crown of interviews, and there was just no way this horse wouldn't take first prize. Our TV interview luck was too great to deny.

The day of the race was perfect; I got to wear a big red fancy hat on *Fox & Friends*, made some Belmont Jewel drinks on television, and got plenty excited leading up to the race. Sean joined me in the afternoon, and we spent our wedding anniversary weekend placing bets and enjoying the perfect weather and our great viewing position in the stands.

The moment Justify crossed the finish line was pure joy. It felt like we had all held our breath for over two minutes as the horses battled it out on Big Sandy, the nickname of the track at Belmont. We all hugged each other, laughed, and screamed after it was over. America came together to watch a beautiful animal gallop to the finish line. My gut tells me that's the last time we're going to see a Triple Crown for many, many years. We'll see.

Solar Eclipse of the Heart . . .

The science geek in me will also add witnessing a once-in-a-lifetime total solar eclipse. This brought back memories from the last big solar eclipse event that happened when I was eight years old. I remember it was the lead story on television for weeks back in my Canadian homeland. Millions of people were going to be part of something that only maybe happens a couple of times in our lifetime!

That terrifying warning that scared the crap out of all of us:

"DON'T LOOK DIRECTLY AT THE SUN DURING A SOLAR ECLIPSE. ANYTIME. YOU WILL GO BLIND!"

A very basic description of an eclipse is when one object in space blocks an observer from seeing another object in space.

A solar eclipse happens when the moon passes in front of the sun, causing a shadow to fall on certain parts of the Earth. The eclipse is not seen from every place on Earth, but only from the locations where the shadow falls and the sun appears to have gone dark.

If the sun is completely covered, that is a total solar eclipse.

Back in 1979, the central shadow of the moon passed through several US states and a few Canadian provinces, including Ontario.

Our teachers were planning lessons about this incredible celestial event. Chalkboard diagrams, planetary mobiles, and handmade viewing devices were being created out of shoeboxes. We were all being prepped for the event of the year.

Thirty-eight years later, the Earth, sun, and moon were doing it again, but this time many more people could experience the total darkness. It was the first coast-to-coast total solar eclipse in ninety-nine years.

I pitched the story to *Fox & Friends*, grabbed my special ISO 12312–2 total solar filter eclipse sunglasses, and flew to Greenville, South Carolina, to broadcast live.

It was awesome. We ended up gathering with a few thousand people at a baseball stadium, and for two minutes the whole city went dark in the middle of the day. There were people crying, laughing, hugging each other. It was a moment where many of us realized we ultimately have no control of what the Earth decides to do. We are all just lucky visitors on this planet, so just enjoy the ride.

It was clear we all had just experienced something amazing together, most of us as strangers. How appropriate that the Great American Eclipse was happening for me where one of America's biggest sports was being played.

And you can bet I'll be planning to be part of the next total solar eclipse. Mark it on your calendar: April 8, 2024.

A Stand-Up Gal!

I've only written one fan letter in my life. It was to Steve Martin, because I think he's one of the funniest men on earth. Not only is he hilarious, but he's thoughtful and incredibly smart. His book *Born Standing Up* is one of my favorites, and I've had a fascination with comedians my entire life. I remember my parents coming home and saying the movie *The Jerk* was one of the funniest things they had ever seen. His "wild and crazy guy" on *Saturday Night Live* was required viewing.

To make people laugh is one of the greatest gifts on earth. I am in awe of people who can stand in front of an audience by themselves and try to bring a smile to someone's face. To make someone laugh is, to me, like cracking a code. So I wrote Steve Martin to tell him how much I admired him and thought he was pure magic. Sadly, I never got a letter back. When I was working at *Imus* one week, someone mentioned Steve Martin was going to be an upcoming guest on the program. When I found out, it was like Christmas. I couldn't wait to meet him in person and maybe get a picture taken with one of my idols. Alas, it wasn't meant to be. My program director told me Steve was very shy and didn't like to meet people. We were told he would be brought in quietly and would speak to Imus and Charles for a few minutes. He was promoting a CD of his banjo music, so he wanted to focus on that. I was crestfallen. Later, I read Steve Martin suffered from panic attacks and hypochondria and was anxious. I had no idea if that was true, but I sure was disappointed I wouldn't get to meet him. The day he came in to WFAN, he just walked in, didn't stop to say hello to anyone, and went straight into the studio. He left as quietly as he came in.

I've read this about many comedians. Even though they look like they are the most social and funniest people in the room, many are often reclusive, quiet, moody, and introverted. Still, I was fascinated by them and their craft. For many years I wondered if I could do what they do: stand up in a room, by myself, and make people laugh.

A few years ago I was given the chance. There's an annual competition here in New York to find the "Funniest Reporter." The organizers thought it would be a great idea to get local and national anchors and reporters to try their luck at stand-up while raising money for charity. I've been to a few Funniest Reporter evenings over the years and had a great time seeing my colleagues and TV competitors try out their best jokes. Some bombed spectacularly, while many of them did very well.

If given the chance, could I do this too? When I emcee or host events, I can usually entertain the crowd and get a few laughs. What about writing jokes and doing a full routine? It was something I certainly fantasized about. So when I got a call from media relations asking if I would be interested in competing, I immediately got butterflies and started to flop sweat. Holy moly. Could I do this? Air bands, school plays, and doing the weather on TV were one thing, but telling jokes to a roomful of people and peers gave me almost a sick feeling in my stomach. I said I would think about it and then I called Sean, who didn't miss a beat:

"Are you kidding? You have to do this. You will crush it! This is something you were born to do."

My husband. He had more faith in me than I did.

I called our media relations team, took a deep breath, and said: "I'll do it."

The organizers of the event set us up with a comedy mentor: someone in the business who would give us a crash course on being funny. My mentor was a sweet, very funny young man named Jonathan Morvay. We agreed to meet for lunch to talk about how he could help me win this competition. In the meantime, he told me to start writing down anything and everything I thought would make an audience laugh. I bought a notebook and started scribbling things down: being a mom, babies, living in New York, being Canadian. I wrote about how adult wine sippy cups should be a thing, my two-year-old seeing my naked butt and comparing it to pizza dough, living in a house with three men and my youngest boy asking if I sat down on the toilet to pee because I was tired.

All of this had possibilities. My mind was racing. I remember waking up in the middle of the night with "funny" ideas. I was even dreaming in stand-up. I had to keep a notebook close to my bed at night. My husband reminds me that I turned into a bit of a crazy person during this time, constantly asking him about things that might be funny. I drove him mad. It was all I could think about.

When I met with Jonathan, we went over my notes. A lot of what I wrote had to do with what I did for a living: being a meteorologist. Jonathan told me I could draw on my experiences as a weather person. I had a treasure trove of material that had possibilities. I began writing the funniest things about doing the weather on television. I started with some of the emails I used to get in the good ol' days, before social media gave us constant feedback on our appearance/presentation and our ability to forecast.

This one comes from a guy who was mad the snow that all of the forecasters were predicting never came:

Hey weather lady, would you like to come shovel your 5 inches of partly cloudy off my driveway? Thanks.

Comments on my appearance while carrying a child:

Dear Janice Dean, when you do the weather your pregnant belly is always in the way of my hometown of Jackson, Mississippi. Please move that thing out of the way.

Isn't that nice? Even now that I'm not pregnant, I try to block the city with my rear end just to piss the guy off.

Comments on the power I have when it comes to backyard plants:

Dear Janice: Just FYI, you killed my rose garden. Signed, SADCAT-LADY47

Personalized forecasts:

Hi Janice Dean, the Weather Machine. Can you tell me if it will rain on my wedding May 24th? (It's dated January 5.)

How about this: Mostly cold with a 50 percent chance of divorce? Ba-da-bum.

By the way, "I hate this weather!" and "Hey Janice, how's the weather in South Carolina where I own several properties?" aren't an appropriate way to greet me in the hallway.

I also talked about the weirdest places I get asked for a weather forecast. The ladies' bathroom is up there, in line at the Dunkin' Donuts, the school bus stop, while I'm getting my hair colored . . . but the weirdest place I was asked for a forecast was my OB-GYN's office during . . . ahem . . . a "tune-up"!

"Hey, Janice, I'm heading to the Hamptons this weekend. Are we looking at rain on Saturday?"

I burst out laughing and told her I would have a look at the forecast radar once I got out of the stirrups.

My final jokes featured the "Top five X-rated weather terms." Stop reading here if you are easily offended! Also, please note that even though the names are true, the added bits of information may or may not be accurate.

5. PANHANDLE HOOKER (slang for a tornado).
4. VERTICALLY ERECT SYSTEM (the positioning of a storm system). "That panhandle hooker loves a vertically erect system."
3. REAR END INFLOW. I usually have to EASE INTO this announcement.
2. BULGING TOP. Hard not to notice this term.

And the number-one X-rated sounding weather term:
Choking downdraft. (Cough cough!)
Thank you, everybody! Good night!

The show was at the Comic Strip in New York and was one of the most out-of-my-comfort-zone things I've ever done. I was genuinely out-of-my-mind nervous leading up to the event. Jonathan was there for moral support along with Sean and a lot of other media people. I had a cheering section from Fox, which I was grateful for. I wanted to have a few drinks to loosen me up, but Jonathan told me to stay sober. I needed to be alert and remember my routine. I could drink a bucket of vodka afterward. It was ultimately good advice, but I had to wait a LOOOOOOONG time to have my first alcoholic beverage because I was the LAST PERFORMER. I had butterflies the whole show until my name was finally called. I don't remember the other routines because I was too busy going over my act throughout everyone's jokes.

Looking back, it was one of the most challenging, rewarding experiences of my life. Standing up in front of an audience and trying to be funny is quite a feat. When you do hear them laugh, it's one of the best rushes you'll ever get as a performer. Jonathan told me that some nights you'll be on top of the world, have a great show where you knew you "killed" with your jokes, and then the next night you might not have any laughs, or you'll have hecklers and you'll want to quit the business.

Once my ten minutes were over, I was relieved but thrilled I had done it. By the way, I tied for first prize with a local reporter who performed a song-and-dance routine while showing off her cleavage in a VERY low-cut top. It was impressive (the singing and dancing), but I felt like she should've entered a best "Broadway show" contest, since I was true to the agenda (pure stand-up) and she colored outside the lines.

Oh, well. It still goes down as being one of the most thrilling things I've ever done. I have the trophy to prove it.

I'm with the Band

My next story is a classic rock dream come true.

A few years ago, we had someone called a "mentalist" on *Fox & Friends* who was able to identify some of our biggest, most personal secrets. Steve Doocy, Brian Kilmeade, and I had to write down something that no one would guess about us, and then we were told to rip it up and throw it away. The mind reader would then announce on live television what we had written down without ever seeing what we wrote. Full disclosure: Steve and I kind of figured out how he did the trick, but that's not the point of the story (although, if you want to know how the trick is done, ask me and I'll whisper it to you). My secret was: I've always wanted to sing in a rock band.

Admittedly, I think I'm an okay singer. I can belt out "These Boots Are Made for Walking" at the karaoke bar. I've been to a few rock shows in my lifetime, even getting onstage to introduce a few bands, so you could surmise I might've liked to do this for a living or in my free time. It was always just kind of a fantasy, something as a teenager I would imagine as I played Bonnie Tyler and lip-synched the words to "Total Eclipse of the Heart" in front of the mirror in my bedroom.

Last summer we had the band Lynyrd Skynyrd playing on the plaza for our All-American Summer Concert Series. If you're a classic rock fan, you know all of their big hits. There are many of them: "Simple Man," "Tuesday's Gone," "Saturday Night Special," "That Smell," "What's Your Name," and "Free Bird." I played all these great tracks as a classic rock DJ back in Ottawa in the '80s.

Their signature song, "Sweet Home Alabama," is one of the most popular rock songs of all time. And I got to sing it onstage for the band's farewell tour, making my little dream of performing with a rock band come true.

I was in the "fishbowl" (the little glass room downstairs from where the famous curvy couch is) in Studio F, working on my daily Dean's List feature on Fox News Radio. When the studio doors opened, three of the band members from Lynyrd Skynyrd walked in to do a "tease" before the commercial break to let everyone know they were going to be playing outside in the next hour of *Fox & Friends*. Johnny Van Zant (Ronnie's brother, who has been the band's lead vocalist since 1987), Gary Rossington (original band member since they formed in the early '70s), and Rickey Medlocke (frontman/guitarist) came in looking like the true rock stars they are. When they saw me, they stopped walking.

"Hey! It's the weather lady! It's the weather lady right here!" said Rickey with his beautiful long white hair in a ponytail and his worn-out leather Skynyrd jacket.

Well, this was something else. They all told me they enjoyed watching me doing the weather. I looked around to see if they were actually talking to me. Rickey added:

"So, the next time you're doing the weather, just remember we're watching you from home in sunny Florida if you ever want to give us a shout-out!"

I may have squealed with delight.

If you've ever seen our show during the summer concert series, you'll always catch me in the crowd no matter who is performing. Music is one of the things that brings people together in this world, and I love watching people forgetting about life for a while and being a part of the audience. So while the guys were playing "Gimme Three Steps" and "That Smell," I was dancing and singing along with the hundreds of people who showed up to fill our little concert pit. Johnny Van Zant even came over to the edge of the stage and grabbed my hand while singing. I could tell he got a kick out of me being a superfan. In between songs, I was going onstage to warm up the crowd and talk to everyone in the audience.

Backstage, the guys joked that I should come on tour with them, since I was so good at talking to the audience and getting them worked up for the next song. I told them to be careful saying something like that. They just might see me sneaking onto the back of their tour bus. I filled them in on my background before doing the weather, playing classic rock in Ottawa. I got to meet the gals who sang backup, better known as the Honkettes: Dale Rossington (married to original Skynyrd member Gary Rossington) and Carol Chase. I have to tell you, the fact that these ladies are still rocking it past their fifties impressed me to no end. They were gorgeous, didn't look like they had a face full of filler or Botox and had stretched their skin back behind their ears. Plus, they sang their asses off and looked like they were having the time of their life.

I decided I wanted to be one of them. Immediately.

I had a big, brilliant idea, so I approached them with it.

"Hey, ladies, would it be okay if I came up and did backup with you during one of the songs?" Without missing a beat, they said:

"Hell, yeah, you can come. We had Pamela Anderson join us one year when she was dating Kid Rock. That woman did things to a microphone we had never seen done before."

I grinned from ear to ear. I was in.

We all got up onstage. I made sure it was okay with the other band members and all of them gave me a thumbs-up. I waved at the crowd while we were waiting for the cue to start playing. People started clapping and cheering. I asked Carol and Dale if there was anything I needed to do in particular while I was dancing with them as their latest backup singer. "Nah, girl. We just make it up sometimes as we go along."

We came back from commercial break, with Steve, Brian, and Ainsley ready to introduce the band . . . and me.

"Welcome back to *Fox & Friends*, everyone. And now, singing one of the biggest songs of all time . . . please welcome Lynyrd Skynyrd and 'Sweet Home Alabama'!"

The stage lights go on and the cameras are on us!

That famous guitar riff began, and then Johnny sang "TURN IT UP!"

I started dancing with the Honkettes, and when we got to the chorus, the girls motioned for me to sing along with them.

It was a moment that's hard to put into words here. You could definitely call it a "bucket list," a dream come true, or just a few minutes of pure joy, singing backup with a famous band, on one of the most beloved songs of all time. I closed my eyes for a second afterward and just took it all in. This was something special.

After the song was over, the band played one more before they hopped on their tour bus. I hugged everyone and told them this was something I would never forget. We took pictures, and the crews began to start tearing down. A.J., who puts together the summer concert series every year, came up to me and told me there were members of the crew who were asking "Who was that energetic lady that was singing backup? She sure looked like she was having fun!" I smiled and yelled, "That was one of the best things I've ever done in my entire life!"

I put it out there in the universe, and it came true.

Seeing Dale and Carol singing and still rocking and rolling onstage gave me hope that maybe I could also keep doing what I love to do well into my fifties. Maybe even into my sixties. Just a few years ago I thought my career was over. Sometimes I feel like I'm just getting started.

It's moments like that that I'm starting to appreciate even more these days. One of the big lessons I've learned in this life so far is to appreciate every moment. Enjoy it. Take chances. Do things that you've dreamed of doing. Get out of your comfort zone sometimes. Write down something on a piece of paper that you've always wanted to do and try to achieve it. We shouldn't need a mentalist to remind us to strive for big things.

I've got a lot more years in this life of mine, and you can bet I'm going to fill them with bucket list moments. Last summer I ziplined through the Colorado Rockies. Before I tried it, I asked the guide the age of the oldest person he had witnessed doing this. He told me seventy-four. I then asked him the heaviest person. He answered: 250 pounds. I inquired if anyone had died recently. He said no. So I was well within the guidelines of age and weight and possibly not dying. When you're standing 90 feet above the ground, and 11,000 feet above sea level, you do question why exactly you are doing something this crazy. Then I thought about my kids. Would they think this was awesome? Oh, yes, they would. You can bet when they fit the height and age requirements, I'll be doing it again—with them by my side.

Sometimes we have to remind ourselves to take a deep breath and jump right in. Sing like you belong in the band. Act like you've always been there. Dance like no one is watching. Or, in my case . . . like *everyone* is watching. I've learned over the years that sometimes you have to make your own sunshine. In life, silver linings can always be found, even in the darkest of moments.

I remember what my dad used to always tell me: Do what you most love to do, and it won't ever feel like work. His advice was right. However, I would add: Do things that also make you happy. Spend time with your family. Allow yourself to be loved. Smile as much as possible. Be kind and considerate. Sometimes one nice gesture can change a person's day.

My dad gave me a poem that he loved before he left. I found it recently in my box of memories I keep under my bed with my baby book and pictures from my childhood. It's called "The Desiderata of Happiness" and was written by Max Ehrmann, an American writer, and published in 1927. It's a beautiful piece. It reminds me of the dad I knew when I was a little girl, pushing me gently on my bike without training wheels for the first time.

He's waiting until I get my rhythm and pacing just right. In my mind's eye my mom is in the background cheering me on with my brother, Craig, holding her hand. My father starts to jog beside me until he thinks I'm finally ready to pedal without his help. He finally lets go and I realize I'm riding by myself for the first time with the wind at my back and the sunshine warming my face. I know they're all watching me, proud of me. What a feeling this is! My legs pedal a little faster, but not so much that I scare myself. I'm smiling as I hear him call out: "Go Pookie, go! You're doing it!" I'm gliding down a path that branches off in a few directions, but I'm not quite ready to test out my brakes or veer off somewhere new—yet.

I imagine myself traveling into the future on an adventure that looks very bright from that bicycle seat. I can't wait to discover what's still to come . . .

"The Desiderata of Happiness"

Go placidly amid the noise and haste, and remember what peace there may be in silence.

As far as possible without surrender be on good terms with all persons. Speak your truth quietly and clearly; and listen to others, even the dull and ignorant; they too have their story.

Avoid loud and aggressive persons, they are vexations to the spirit. If you compare yourself with others, you may become vain and bitter; for always there will be greater and lesser persons than yourself. Enjoy your achievements as well as your plans.

Keep interested in your career, however humble; it is a real possession in the changing fortunes of time. Exercise caution in your business affairs; for the world is full of trickery. But let this not blind you to what virtue there is; many persons strive for high ideals; and everywhere life is full of heroism.

Be yourself. Especially, do not feign affection. Neither be cynical about love; for in the face of all aridity and disenchantment it is as perennial as the grass.

Take kindly the counsel of the years, gracefully surrendering the things of youth. Nurture strength of spirit to shield you in sudden misfortune. But do not distress yourself with imaginings. Many fears are born of fatigue and loneliness. Beyond a wholesome discipline, be gentle with yourself.

You are a child of the universe, no less than the trees and the stars;
*   you have a right to be here. And whether or not it is clear to you,*
*   no doubt the universe is unfolding as it should.*
Therefore be at peace with God, whatever you conceive Him to be, and
*   whatever your labors and aspirations, in the noisy confusion of life*
*   keep peace with your soul.*
With all its sham, drudgery and broken dreams, it is still a beautiful
*   world.*
Be cheerful.
Strive to be happy.

ACKNOWLEDGMENTS

After my editor, Eric Nelson, read the chapters I submitted to him for *Mostly Sunny* he told me my story reminded him of a formula that was used by Joseph Campbell called the "Hero's Journey." Some of the greatest stories of all time have been created using Campbell's process. (*Star Wars*, Harry Potter, Spiderman, *The Lion King*, and *The Lord of the Rings*).

During a hero's journey, it's implied that you can never be at peace with yourself if you do not answer the call for adventure. Instead, you can only build up resentment in the knowledge that you missed the opportunity to pursue your purpose. Campbell says: "If you do follow your bliss, you put yourself on a kind of track that has been there all the while, waiting for you, and the life that you ought to be living is the one you are living. I say, follow your bliss and don't be afraid, and doors will open where you didn't know they were going to be."

The main message is to follow your intuition. Embrace the unknown rather than fear it. "We must let go of the life we have planned, so as to accept the one that is waiting for us."

I have always lived my life thinking that we have many paths we can choose to go on, but I have made decisions based on my gut instinct or intuition, believing that fate will ultimately decide the journey. For me, that path was to meet my husband, Sean, and have our family. Every job I've taken, every challenge I went through, ultimately led me to him. But it wasn't until after we met and got married that I realized all the choices and decisions were predestined.

I was flattered that Eric thought my life resembled something of a Hero. But as I read more about Campbell's theory, I now feel it has more to do with the people the Hero meets along the way who help him or her complete the journey.

The helpers. The mentors. The goddesses. The angels here on earth. Looking back, there are so many of these special people—those that lent a hand or gave me encouragement when I needed it most. *Thank you* doesn't begin to describe my gratitude. And I may forget to mention some of you here, but please know there are literally thousands of good people who in some way have changed my life—even with the simplest gestures like a smile or a word of advice. Those subtle moments can make a big difference and perhaps influence a choice that leads us down our ultimate path. Like a butterfly that flaps its tiny wings and somehow might be able to change a weather pattern thousands of miles away. . .

It starts with my family: To Matthew and Theodore who gave me the greatest gift of being your mama. To Sean, I look forward to the rest of our journey together.

My mom, Stella, who from the beginning was always there, and who I get my strength and resilience from.

To my brother, Craig, thank you for putting up with your big sister and being a wonderful uncle to Matthew and Theodore. You and Aunt Liz make my boys light up when you're in the room.

To Mickey and Dee, for raising an amazing son. And being great grandparents to Matthew and Theodore.

To Neera Malhotra. Madame, thank you for always being there, and for the laughs. We always find something funny to smile about even in the most challenging moments.

To Dervla Geary, for being one of my first *Sunny* readers and first neighbors, and my partner in Irish gin. Thanks to you, Paul, and Aoife, for being just a phone call away when things don't go as planned.

DebiAn, it is such a comfort knowing you have helped raise my boys to be sweet, smart, happy people.

Jane Skinner, you continue to be one of my biggest cheerleaders. And you make a mean chocolate chip cookie.

Jen Smrtka, my angel in a white coat. And my wonderful doctors and friends Dr. DeAngelis, Dr. Tullman, and Dr. Waterstone. Thank you for your care and, more important, for caring.

Lianne Laing and Tony Harris. The world's greatest matchmakers. Thank you for letting Sean join in on your honeymoon adventure and starting my fairy-tale ending.

Judy Bristol, who knows me better than anyone. Thank you for listening and for the hugs.

My mentor, teacher, and friend Donna Leon. Thanks for believing in me and fighting for what's right.

To Suzanne Scott and Lauren Petterson, who encouraged me to write my story. The whole story. This book would not be as open and honest without your support and blessing.

My dear friend and superhero Neil Cavuto. Thank you for always having your door open and Kleenex handy.

To Megyn Kelly, Uncle Doug, Yates, Yardley, and Thatcher. Friends are the family we choose for ourselves. Thank you for being a part of our lives.

To Meghan McCain, you're always there for me—whenever I need you. Thank you for always checking in. Call me later!

Abby Huntsman, one of my first *Sunny* readers, I am grateful for your unwavering support. I adore you and your family.

Shannon Bream, I am grateful for your friendship, encouragement, prayers, and love.

Mark Arezzi, Jen Liang, Luke, and Justine. Thank you for standing up for us at our wedding and in life.

My friend Gavin Hadden, for always fighting for the weather report and being a great team leader.

My safe harbors in Houston, Karen and George McCracken, who picked me up and took good care of me.

To Allison Parsons, Patty, and Ian McBean, for also being there when I needed you most.

To Brandon Noriega, who helps keep my forecasts accurate on TV and in all my books. You're a wonderful friend and fantastic senior producer!

To my weather team and good friends Rick Reichmuth and Adam Klotz. Rick has the best umbrella in the business for those "mostly rainy" days. Check it out: weathermanumbrella.com

To Bob Barnett, for your council and friendship, and for introducing *Freddy the Frogcaster* to your grandkids.

To Deneen Howell, for also helping *Freddy* and *Sunny* shine!

Irena Briganti, you've always been in my corner. I appreciate your hard work, dedication, and loyalty.

Jaclyn Giuliano, you always bring a smile to everything you do.

Dianne Brandi, thank you for being kind, fair, and supportive from day one.

Lynne Jordal Martin, for your supportive emails and prayers.

Lily Claffee and Anthony Constantine, for your suggestions and guidance on a tight deadline. And for helping me tell my story openly and honestly.

To Uncle Tommy and Aunt Michele Greco. Your family has helped ours in so many ways. We love you.

My Regnery Kids family who believed in a forecasting frog.

Peter and Cheryl Barnes and Chuck Leavell, for helping me dust off my children's book idea. By the way, check out Mr. Leavell's awesome book *The Tree Farmer* and his website, Mother Nature Network at www.mnn.com

Russ Cox, who made Freddy come to life with his brilliant illustrations.

Governor John Kasich, for giving me one of the greatest ideas of my career in the hallway at Fox.

To Eric Nelson, the kind editor that asked if I might have an adult book in me. I'm grateful for your faith in my writing skills and the encouragement through it all. The HarperCollins family: Eric Meyers, Leslie Cohen, Katie O'Callaghan, Nate Knaebel, and James Iacobelli.

To Bob Cowan, the man who turned on the microphone and gave me my first on-air audition.

Dave Schutte, who gave wonderful advice and support for the beginning years of my broadcasting career.

Mike Giunta, for your kindness and the job recommendation that changed my life. Sorry if I missed playing a CanCon song or two . . .

Mrs. Klein, thank you for your courage to inspire and make a difference. You helped me talk to my boys about having MS. It's a gift I will never forget.

Kevin Magee, you are one of the good ones. I'll never forget your email offering to rescue me from Astoria.

Bethany Mandel, for your brilliant social media commentary and introducing Freddy to your kids #superfrogcasterfans.

To Nicole Treitz, for your beautiful letter and to your husband, Justin, for connecting us. I can't wait to meet you and give you a big hug.

Jonathan Morvay, my standup mentor and all-around fun guy to have lunch with.

To my silent army of women who risked so much to help make it a safer, stronger workplace at Fox News and beyond. I am so proud of all of you.

To my *Fox & Friends* family—especially the team behind the scenes who make it so much fun waking up dark and early.

My hair and makeup teams through the years, thank goodness for our beauticians and magicians, past and present. Especially Alexis and Fouzia who went out of their way to help me find the best job of my life.

One last thing, I wouldn't be writing this book without my *Fox & Friends* viewers. I feel like a lucky lady joining you every morning. I look forward to sharing more smiles, laughs, and plenty of dancing in the years to come. Thank you for reading my "mostly sunny" stories.

Grateful, thankful, blessed.

JD

ABOUT THE AUTHOR

JANICE DEAN is the senior meteorologist at Fox News and serves as the morning meteorologist on *Fox & Friends*. She lives in New York City.